STEP-BY-STEP

50 Delicious Noodle Dishes

STEP-BY-STEP
50 Delicious
Noodle Dishes

Consultant Editor: Christine Ingram

LORENZ BOOKS

First published in 1998 by Lorenz Books

© Anness Publishing Limited 1998

Lorenz Books is an imprint of
Anness Publishing Limited
Hermes House
88–89 Blackfriars Road
London SE1 8HA

ISBN 1 85967 739 8

A CIP catalogue record for this book is available from the British Library

Publisher: Joanna Lorenz
Senior Cookery Editor: Linda Fraser
Editor: Margaret Malone
Designer: Lilian Lindblom
Photographers: Karl Adamson, Edward Allwright, Steve Baxter,
James Duncan, Amanda Heywood, Tim Hill and Don Last
Recipes: Alex Barker, Carla Capalbo, Christine France, Sarah Gates,
Shirley Gill, Patricia Lousada, Norma MacMillan, Sue Maggs,
Sarah Maxwell, Janice Murfitt, Angela Nilsen, Hilaire Walden,
Laura Washburn, Steven Wheeler and Elizabeth Wolf-Cohen.

For all recipes, quantities are given in both metric and imperial
measures and, where appropriate, measures are also given in standard
cups and spoons. Follow one set, but not a mixture, because they are
not interchangeable.

Printed in Hong Kong/China

1 3 5 7 9 10 8 6 4 2

CONTENTS

INTRODUCTION

Noodles are loved the world over and are used in countless recipes. Thanks to Marco Polo, noodles have an undisputed place in western kitchens, but this book concentrates on the noodle dishes of Asia. China, Thailand, Japan and Indonesia, together with Vietnam, Burma and Malaysia, have their own traditional noodle dishes and many of these have become as popular in the west as they are in their own countries. Chow mein, Singapore Noodles, Thai Fried Noodles and Sukiyaki from Japan are now among our own favourites and are just a few of the many superb dishes featured in this book.

Unlike Italian pasta, which is produced almost exclusively from wheat, Asian noodles are also made from rice, pea starch and even from arrowroot, generally depending on the principal crop of the region. Wheat noodles are one of the staple foods of northern China, where wheat is the primary grain. These are made with or without egg and are sold in a huge variety of widths, from fine vermicelli strands to thick and broad ribbons. Rice noodles, characterized by their opaque, pale colour, also come in a range of widths, while cellophane noodles are thin and wiry, used for soups or adding to vegetable dishes.

In many cuisines, noodles play an important role in traditional festivities. In China they are a symbol of longevity, eaten at birthdays and weddings and as 'crossing of the threshold of the year' food. They are also a favourite snack food, sold on the street, tossed simply with flavoured oils, garlic or ginger or served with meat and vegetables. Noodles are the original fast food in the East, sold everywhere and for everyone at any time of the day. This book offers a selection of all types of noodle dishes, from soups and snacks to main meals for the family and special occasions.

Types of Noodle

The range of Asian noodles is extensive, from fine and thin to coarse and thick, made of wheat flour (with or without egg), rice flour or vegetable starch, and available fresh or dried. They are amazingly versatile.

Chinese noodles

Depending on the region and therefore on locally grown produce, Chinese noodles are made from one of three main ingredients – wheat flour, rice flour or mung beans. They come in a variety of shapes and thicknesses, often tied into bundles with raffia, or coiled into squares or oblongs. They are traditionally long, as this is believed to symbolize a long life.

Although most South East Asian countries produce their own noodles, Chinese-style noodles can be used for any of the speciality dishes from Malaysia, Indonesia and Thailand. Like pasta, most noodles are interchangeable, and if a certain type or thickness of noodle isn't available, a similar one can be used instead. The exception is cellophane noodles, which are used more as a vegetable to give texture to a dish, rather than as a staple.

Wheat noodles

These come from northern China where wheat is the principal grain. Pure wheat noodles are often packaged like Italian spaghetti, in long thin sticks, or wound into nests.

Egg noodles

Egg noodles are the most common and most versatile of all Chinese noodles. They are made from wheat with egg added, giving the characteristic yellow colour. Fresh egg noodles, such as those used for chow mein, are becoming increasingly available, not only in Chinese stores, but also in most large supermarkets. They are usually sold in thick coils and resemble balls of wool.

Dried egg noodles are normally coiled into compressed squares or oblongs. They come in a variety of thicknesses, from the thin, thread-like noodles, to broad, thick strips, and they can be ribbon-shaped or rounded.

Fresh noodles, like fresh pasta, have a better flavour and texture, but for cooking times check the packet instructions, as these will depend on their thickness. Dried noodles are best soaked briefly in warm water to untangle before adding to your dish.

Cellophane, Mung bean or Pea starch noodles

These are made from ground mung beans and are also known as bean thread, transparent or glass noodles. They are thin and wiry and sold in bundles tied with a thread, but unlike rice vermicelli, they are translucent and are not brittle, and can only be broken up using scissors.

The dried noodles need to be soaked before cooking, and then can be used in soups and other dishes with plenty of sauce or stock, as they absorb four times their weight in liquid.

In a continent where texture is as important as flavour, these slippery-textured noodles are very popular, and while they have little or no flavour of their own, they will take on the flavours of other ingredients.

Rice noodles

Made from ground rice, these come from southern parts of China, where rice is the staple crop. They range in thickness from very thin to wide ribbons and sheets. Dried ribbon rice noodles are usually sold tied together in bundles or come coiled into square packages.

Rice vermicelli

Made from rice flour, these noodles are very thin, white and brittle, and are sold in large bundles, often tied with cotton or raffia. They should be soaked briefly and will then cook almost instantly in hot liquid. In their dried form they can be deep-fried for crispy noodles – don't soak them first.

plain flour noodles

fresh medium egg noodles

rice vermicelli

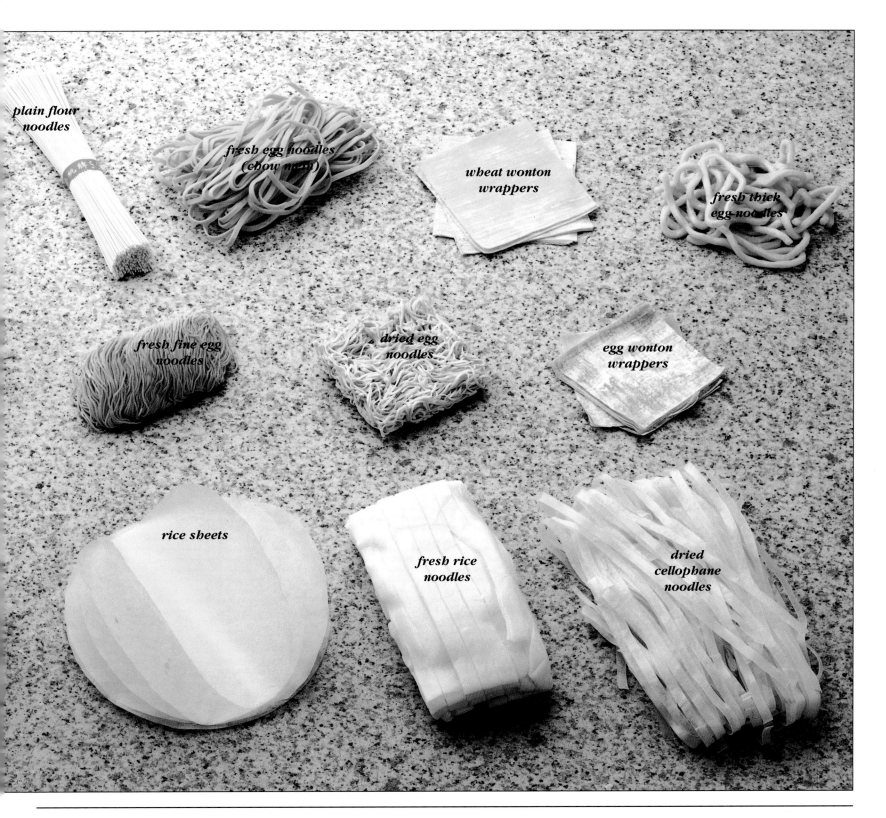

plain flour noodles

fresh egg noodles (chow mein)

wheat wonton wrappers

fresh thick egg-noodles

fresh fine egg noodles

dried egg noodles

egg wonton wrappers

rice sheets

fresh rice noodles

dried cellophane noodles

Japanese noodles

There are four main types of Japanese noodle, all of which play an important part in its cuisine. Although distinct from Chinese noodles, they share many of the same characteristics, and most Japanese noodles are available from Chinese supermarkets, where they are as popular in Chinese cuisine as they are in Japan.

Gyoza wrappers

The Japanese equivalent to wonton skins. The wrappers can be filled with ground meat, fish, vegetables and seasonings. They are usually browned on one side, turned and simmered in broth and served as appetizers.

Harusame noodles

Meaning "spring rain", these transparent noodles are the equivalent to the Chinese cellophane noodles. They can be deep-fried, or soaked and are used in a variety of dishes.

Soba noodles

Made from a mixture of buckwheat and wheat flour, these noodles are very popular in Japan. Thin and brownish in colour, they are used in soups and are sometimes served cold with garnishes and a dipping sauce. They are best cooked in simmering water for a few minutes, until tender.

Somen noodles

These are very fine, white noodles made from wheat flour. They come dried, usually tied in bundles, held together with a paper band.

They are ideal in soups, in the popular Japanese one-pot meals and are also often served cold as a summer dish. If they are not available, vermicelli pasta can be used instead.

Udon noodles

These are the most popular and versatile of Japanese noodles. Like somen noodles, they are made from white wheat flour but are thicker and more substantial. They are normally rounded in shape like spaghetti, although they can be flat.

Udon noodles are available fresh, pre-cooked or dried. Fresh noodles need only a few minutes' cooking in simmering water, for noodles straight from the packet, follow the directions provided. Udon noodles are generally served in hot soups and in mixed meat and vegetable dishes.

Other noodles: River rice noodles

Made from rice ground with water, these Chinese noodles have been steamed into thin sheets before being cut into ribbons about 1 cm/$\frac{1}{2}$ in wide. They can be used in stir-fries or chow mein dishes. If possible, buy fresh noodles, as they have an excellent flavour and texture. Dried noodles should be boiled and drained before use.

Spring roll wrappers

Thinner and larger than wonton wrappers, these are made from wheat flour and water. There are two types, the Cantonese, which are smooth, like a noodle dough, and the Shanghai, which are transparent, like rice paper.

Wonton wrappers

These are made from the same dough as egg noodles, namely wheat flour, egg and water, cut into circles and 7.5 cm/3 in squares of varying thicknesses. They are normally sold fresh or frozen; if frozen, they will keep for several months.

Gyoza wrappers

somen noodles

NOODLE KNOW-HOW

Dried noodles should be stored in airtight containers, where they can be kept for many months. Fresh noodles will keep in the fridge for 3–4 days, or in an unopened packet until their use-by date. They can also be frozen for up to 6 months.

Quantities will depend not only on appetite but also on whether there are accompanying noodle or rice dishes. If noodles are the principal dish, allow 75–115 g/3–4 oz fresh noodles or one square or oblong of dried noodles per person. The exception is cellophane noodles, which are used more as a vegetable and therefore quantities will generally be smaller. Cellophane noodles may need presoaking for 30 minutes.

spring roll
wrappers

dried soba
noodles

fresh soba
noodles

dried udon
noodles

fresh udon noodles

Harusame
noodles

Fresh and Store-cupboard Essentials

Almost all ingredients you can think of – and many you wouldn't – can be used in noodle dishes. Many of the traditional oriental ingredients are available in supermarkets or in Asian grocers, so it is possible to make dishes from the East that are absolutely authentic.

Bamboo shoots
These are available fresh but are more commonly seen canned. They have a fairly bland flavour and are generally used for their crunchy texture. Drain well and rinse under cold water before using in a recipe.

Beancurd/Tofu
This soya bean product is available in several forms, including soft, firm, silken, grilled, fried and dried. Plain, uncooked beancurd is entirely neutral in taste, absorbing the flavour of other ingredients.

It is low in fat, high in protein and calcium and is therefore a versatile and useful ingredient for healthy, low-calorie meals.

Beancurd cheese/Red-fermented beancurd
This deep red beancurd has a very strong and cheesy flavour. It is fermented with salt, red rice and rice wine and is used in Asian cooking for flavouring meat, poultry and vegetarian dishes. It is usually stored in jars or earthenware pots and will keep for several months if refrigerated.

Beansprouts
Used for their delicious texture in meat and vegetable dishes, cook for only 30 seconds. They will keep for 1–2 days in the fridge, but will discolour and wilt if left any longer.

Black beans, fermented
These whole soya beans are preserved in salt and ginger. They are pungent in taste but, when cooked in stir-fries or other dishes with additional ingredients, bring a delicious flavour to the meal.

Bonito
In Japanese cookery, these are the dried flakes of a strongly flavoured tuna. They are used frequently for stocks and soups and can be sprinkled over food as a seasoning.

Chinese leaves/Chinese lettuce
The crispy leaves of this vegetable are ideal for stir-frying or for soups. They are particularly popular in the latter, where their crunchy texture contrasts wonderfully with cellophane noodles.

Chinese mushrooms
These add flavour and texture to numerous Asian dishes. They are almost always sold dried and should be soaked before using. The caps are then sliced or halved, the stems discarded.

Cloud ears
These Chinese mushrooms are only available dried. After soaking they expand to form thick, brown clusters. They have little or no flavour, absorbing flavours from other seasonings, but are appreciated for their silky but crunchy texture. Rinse well to remove any sand and discard any hard bits.

Coconut milk/Coconut cream
Used in almost all Asian cuisine, coconut milk is especially popular in Thai, Indonesian and Malaysian cooking, where it is used extensively, particularly in fish and poultry dishes.

Cans of coconut milk and cream are available from most supermarkets, as well as oriental stores. Buy unsweetened coconut milk. If the recipe calls for sugar, add this yourself.

Creamed coconut is a solid bar of milky-white coconut, which will keep in the fridge for months. Dissolve it in hot or boiling water according to the packet directions.

Dashi
The name given to the Japanese kombu and bonito stock. Instant dashi is available from Japanese and most large Chinese grocers.

Enoki mushrooms
These small, cultivated mushrooms have long, thin stems and tiny, white caps. They are harvested in clumps attached at the base, which should be cut off before use. They have a crisp texture and delicate flavour and may be eaten raw or lightly cooked. When using in cooked dishes, add at the last minute, as heating tends to toughen them.

Fish sauce
This is an essential ingredient in many South East Asian countries, particularly Thailand and Indonesia.

Made from the liquid from salted fermented anchovies, it has a strong aroma and taste. Use sparingly until you acquire the taste.

Kombu
This popular Japanese ingredient is a type of kelp seaweed and is used to flavour stock. Kombu and bonito flake stock granules are available from Japanese supermarkets, as is a liquid form and a teabag-style instant stock. Kombu can also be served as a vegetable.

Mooli
Also known as daikon or Chinese radish, this large, white vegetable has a smooth, creamy-white skin and is normally sold with feathery, green tops. It has a pleasant, slightly spicy taste and is excellent steamed, pickled, used in stir-fries and chow mein or thinly sliced and eaten raw.

Mustard greens/ Mustard cabbage

There are many varieties of mustard greens but the most commonly available and most suitable for cooking, rather than pickling, are those with a pale green stalk and large, single, oval leaf. They have a very distinctive taste and are used in soups and thick stews.

Nori/Yaki-nori/Ao-nori

Nori is dried seaweed, popular in Japanese and some Thai cooking. It is sold in paper-thin sheets which are dark green to black in colour. It is normally toasted and used as a wrapping for sushi and as a garnish.

Yaki-nori are ready-toasted sheets and ao-nori is a flaked, dried green seaweed used for seasoning. Both are available from oriental stores.

Oil

The favoured oil in most Asian cooking is groundnut or peanut oil. It has a rich, nutty flavour. However, it is expensive and not widely available and corn oil or sunflower oil can be used as a satisfactory substitute.

Sesame oil, with its distinct, nutty flavour, is made from toasted sesame seeds and is used for stirring into noodles or sprinkling over noodle dishes. It burns easily and is not recommended for cooking; however, a little will add a wonderful, aromatic flavour.

Right: Just some of the fresh ingredients used in Asian cooking available in large supermarkets.

Pak choi

This attractive, cabbage-like vegetable has a long, smooth, milky-white stem and large, dark green leaves.

Rice vinegar

This is a pale vinegar with a distinct but delicate flavour. It is milder than most other light wine vinegars and is available from oriental stores.

Rice wine

Chinese rice wine has a rich, sherry-like flavour and is used in marinades or added to stir-fries or fried noodle dishes. It is available from most large super-markets and oriental grocers.

Sake

This Japanese rice wine is now widely available. It is used occasionally in marinades or at the end of cooking and is frequently served, either hot or chilled, with Japanese meals.

Shiitake mushrooms

These tasty, firm-textured Japanese mushrooms are available fresh or dried. They have a meaty, slightly acidic flavour and a rather slippery texture. Dried mushrooms should be soaked in hot water for about 20 minutes and then strained. Save the water for the sauce. Add to stir-fries for a delicious flavour and texture.

Wood ears

These are similar to cloud ears, though larger in size and coarser in texture. Mild in flavour they absorb the taste of the more strongly flavoured ingredients and are used mainly in soups and stir-fries, adding texture and colour.

Yard-long beans

These are long, thin beans, similar to French beans but three or four times longer. Cut into smaller lengths and use just like ordinary beans.

Available in most oriental stores, choose those that are small and flexible. They can be refrigerated for up to five days.

Herbs, Spices and Flavourings

Try to keep a selection of these ingredients handy, so that you can rustle up a quick and delicious noodle dish without extensive shopping.

Chillies

There is a wide range of fresh and dried chillies from which to choose. Generally the larger the chilli, the milder the flavour, although there are exceptions, so be warned!

Chinese chives

Also known as garlic chives, these have larger leaves than normal chives and have a mild garlic flavour. They need very little cooking, so stir them into a dish just before serving or use raw as a garnish. Look for plump, uniformly green specimens with no brown spots.

Coriander

Fresh coriander has a distinct flavour, adding an essential pungency to many Chinese or Indonesian-style dishes. Finely or roughly chop and add to a dish, just before serving, or use as a garnish. Bunches of leaves will keep for up to 5 days in a jar of water.

Cumin

Available as whole seed or ground, cumin has a pungent flavour and is used widely in beef dishes and other dishes requiring a curry flavour. Store in a cool, dark place for no more than six months.

Dried shrimps

Not to be confused with our own prawns, these are small, shelled shrimps that have been salted and dried in the sun. They have a strong, fishy taste and are used as a seasoning for meat and vegetables in Chinese, Thai and Indonesian cooking. Rinse under cold water before use.

Dried shrimp paste or Shrimp sauce

Made from ground shrimps fermented in brine, this has a strong aroma and flavour and is used in Chinese, Thai and Malaysian cuisine to enhance seafood dishes. It is usually sold in jars and will keep almost indefinitely in a cool place.

Five-spice powder

A pungent mixture of cloves, cinnamon, fennel, star anise and Szechuan pepper, used extensively in Chinese cooking.

Galangal

This rhizome is reminiscent of ginger, pine and citrus and is similar in appearance to ginger, except that it is thinner and the young shoots are bright pink.

Peel in the same way as fresh root ginger and add to sauces and curries. Remove from the dish before serving.

Ginger

This is another essential ingredient in Asian cookery, used for its warm, fresh flavour and pleasant spiciness. Fresh root ginger is widely available and cannot be substituted with ground ginger. Choose ginger with a firm, unblemished skin, peel with a sharp knife and then finely chop or grate according to the recipe.

Kaffir lime leaves

Also known simply as lime leaves, these add a unique flavour and are excellent in marinades, as well as stir-fries and sauces. The leaves need to be bruised to release the flavour, by rubbing between your fingers. If fresh leaves are not available, dried leaves can be used instead.

Lemon grass

This aromatic herb has a thin, tapering stem and a citrusy, verbena flavour. To use, thinly slice the bulb end of the root and add to marinades or sauces according to the recipe.

Mirin

Sweet cooking sake, this has a delicate flavour and is usually added in the final stages of cooking.

Seven-flavour spice or Shichimi

Used in Japanese cooking, this has a noticeably oriental tang. It is made of sansho, seaweed, chilli, tangerine peel, poppy seeds and white and black sesame seeds.

Soy sauce

Made from fermented soya beans, together with salt, sugar and yeast, this is one of the most ancient and popular seasonings in oriental cookery. There are three main types: Chinese dark or thick soy sauce and light or thin soy sauce, and Japanese soy sauce.

Dark soy sauce, which gives a reddish-brown hue to food, is used for meatier 'red-braised' dishes. Light soy sauce is thinner in consistency and paler in colour. It still has a salty flavour, but is used for paler dishes, such as chicken or fish. Japanese soy sauce (also called shoyu) is lighter in flavour than Chinese soy sauces and is best used when making the more delicate Japanese food.

Star anise

This spice has a pungent, aniseed flavour and is used either ground or whole.

Szechuan chilli paste/ Chilli paste

This hot paste of dried red chillies and ground yellow bean sauce is wonderful in fish dishes.

Tamarind

The brown, sticky pulp of the bean-like seed pod of the tamarind tree. The pulp is usually diluted with water and strained before use. Tamarind has a sour, yet fruity taste, resembling sour prunes.

Right: Experiment with the wonderful array of Asian herbs and spices available today.

Equipment

You will find most of the cooking equipment you have around the kitchen will be all you need. A wok is probably the most useful item, although even that is not essential, as a large frying pan can be substituted. However, if you are interested in investing in authentic tools of the trade, consider some of the following:

Bamboo skewers

These are widely used for barbecues and grilled foods. They should be soaked before use, and then discarded afterwards.

Chopping board

A good-quality chopping board with a thick surface is essential and will last for years.

Citrus zester

This tool is designed to remove the rind or zest of citrus fruit, while leaving the bitter white pith. It can also be used for shaving fresh coconut.

Cleaver

The weight of the cleaver makes it ideal for chopping all kinds of ingredients. Keep this as sharp as possible.

Cooking chopsticks

These are extra-long and allow you to stir ingredients in the wok while keeping a safe distance.

Draining wire

This is designed to sit on the side of the wok and is used mainly when deep-frying.

Food processor

Useful for numerous kitchen tasks, this is a quick alternative to the pestle and mortar.

Knives

It is very important to use the right-sized knife for the job, for safety and for efficiency. There are two essential knives that should be in every kitchen. A chopping knife with a heavy, wide blade about 18–20 cm/ 7–8 in long is ideal for chopping vegetables, meats and fresh herbs. A paring knife has a smaller blade and is necessary for trimming and peeling vegetables and fruits.

Ladle

A long-handled ladle is very useful for spooning out soups, stock and sauces.

Pestle and mortar

A deep granite pestle and mortar is ideal for crushing garlic, ginger and herbs to a paste or for grinding small amounts of spices.

Rice paddle

Used to fluff up rice after cooking.

Saucepan

A good saucepan with a tight-fitting lid is essential for cooking rice properly.

Sharpening stone

A traditional tool for sharpening knives and cleavers. It is available from hardware stores.

Stainless-steel skimmer

This can be used when strong flavours are likely to affect bare-metal cooking implements.

Wire skimmer

This is the Asian alternative to a slotted spoon and one or the other is absolutely essential in Asian cooking. Use for removing cooked food from boiling water or hot fat. However, it should not be used with fish-based liquids as the strong flavour is likely to react with the metal.

Wok

The shape of the wok allows ingredients to be cooked in a minimum of fat, thus retaining freshness and flavour. There are several varieties available, including the carbon-steel, round-bottomed or Pau wok. A round-bottomed wok is best suited to a gas hob, where you will be able to control the amount of heat needed more easily. The carbon-steel, flat-bottomed wok is best for electric or solid-fuel hobs as it gives a better heat distribution.

Warm the wok gently before adding the oil for cooking. The oil then floods easily over the warm pan and prevents food from sticking.

wok

cooking chopsticks

stainless-steel skimmers

food processor

bamboo skewers

saucepan

chopping
board

chopping
knife

draining
wire

sharpening
stone

citrus
zester

cleavers

pestle and
mortar

rice paddle

wire skimmer

BASIC TECHNIQUES

Preparing Lemon Grass

Use the whole stem and remove it before cooking or chop the root.

1 Cut off and discard the dry, leafy tops. Peel away any tough outer layers. Trim off the tops and end of the stem until you are left with about 10 cm/4 in.

2 Lay the lemon grass on a board. Set the flat side of a chef's knife on top and strike it firmly with your fist. Cut across the lemon grass to make thin slices.

Preparing Kaffir Lime Leaves

The distinctive lime-lemon aroma and flavour of Kaffir lime leaves are a vital part of Thai cooking.

COOK'S TIP
Buy fresh lime leaves in oriental stores and freeze them for future use. Dried lime leaves are also now available.

1 You can tear, shred or cut kaffir lime leaves. Using a small, sharp knife, carefully remove the centre vein. Cut the leaves crossways into very fine strips.

Preparing Fresh Ginger

Fresh root ginger can be used in slices, strips or finely chopped.

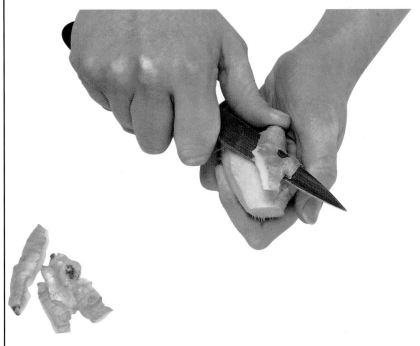

1 Using a small, sharp knife, peel the skin from the root ginger.

2 Place the ginger on a board, set the flat side of a cleaver or chef's knife on top and strike it firmly with your fist – this will soften the fibrous texture.

3 Chop the ginger as coarsely or finely as you wish, moving the blade backwards and forwards.

Preparing Beansprouts

Usually available from supermarkets, beansprouts add a crisp texture to stir-fries.

1 Pick over the beansprouts, discarding any pieces that are discoloured, broken or wilted.

2 Rinse the beansprouts under cold running water and drain well.

Preparing Spring Onions

Use spring onions in stir-fries to flavour oil, as a vegetable in their own right, or as a garnish.

1 Trim off the root and any discoloured tops with a sharp knife. For an intense flavour in a stir-fry, cut the entire spring onion into thin matchsticks.

2 Alternatively, slice the white and pale green part of the spring onion diagonally and stir-fry with crushed garlic, to flavour the cooking oil.

Chopping Coriander

Chop coriander just before you use it, the flavour will then be much better.

1 Strip the leaves from the stalks and pile them on a chopping board.

2 Using a cleaver or chef's knife, cut the coriander into small pieces, moving the blade back and forth until it is as coarsely or finely chopped as you wish.

Preparing Chillies

The flavour of chilli is wonderful in cooking, but fresh chillies must be handled with care.

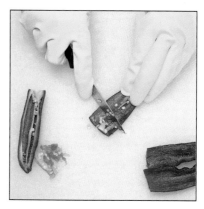

1 Wearing rubber gloves, remove the stalks from the chillies.

2 Cut in half lengthways. Scrape out the seeds and fleshy, white pith from each half, using a sharp knife. Chop or thinly slice according to the recipe.

Seasoning a Wok

If you are using a new wok or frying pan, you will need to prepare it as follows, to ensure the best results described below.

1 A brand new wok will probably have been given a protective coating of oil by the manufacturer, which will need to be removed before seasoning. To do this, scrub the wok with a cream cleanser, rinse thoroughly and dry.

To season the wok, place it over a low heat and add 30 ml/2 tbsp vegetable oil. Using a pad of kitchen paper, rub the entire inside of the wok with the oil, then heat slowly for 10–15 minutes.

2 Using a pad of kitchen paper, rub the entire inside of the wok with the oil, then heat slowly for 10–15 minutes.

3 Alternatively add 30–45 ml/2–3 tbsp salt to the wok and heat slowly for the same length of time.

4 Wipe the inside of the wok clean with more kitchen paper; the paper will become black. Repeat the process of coating, heating and wiping several times until the paper is no longer blackened. The wok is now seasoned and will have a good non-stick surface; do not scrub it again.

COOK'S TIP

To keep a seasoned wok clean, just wash it in hot water without detergent, then wipe it dry. The wok may rust if not in constant use. If it does, scour the rust off and repeat the seasoning process.

Deep-frying

The advantage of a wok is that it can be used for deep-frying as well as stir-frying. It uses far less oil than a deep fat fryer.

1 Put the wok on a stand and half fill with oil. Heat until the required temperature registers on a thermometer. Alternatively, test by dropping in a small piece of food: if bubbles form all over the surface, the oil is ready.

2 Carefully add the food to the oil using long wooden chopsticks or tongs, and move it around to prevent it sticking together. Using a bamboo strainer or slotted spoon, carefully remove the food and drain on kitchen paper before serving. Make sure that the wok is fully secure on its stand before adding the oil. Never leave the wok unattended.

Stir-frying

Many noodle recipes, such as chow mein, involve stir-frying. A wok is the perfect piece of equipment for this type of cooking.

1 Prepare all the ingredients before you start cooking, using a small, sharp knife to cut the vegetables into even-sized pieces. Meat should be cut into thin slices against the grain. It may be easier to slice meat if it has been frozen slightly for an hour or so beforehand. By the time you have sliced it, the meat will be ready to cook.

2 Cutting all the ingredients to a uniform size often means that the preparation of ingredients for stir-frying may take longer than the cooking itself. Once ready, it is important to make sure that all the ingredients are close to hand as wok cooking needs constant attention. Heat the wok for a few minutes before adding the oil.

3 When the pan is hot, add the oil and swirl it or brush it around to coat the base and sides of the wok. Allow the oil to heat for a few moments.

4 Reduce the heat a little, as you add the first ingredients, to ensure they do not burn and that aromatics, like garlic and spring onions, do not become bitter. Stir-fry over quite a high heat, but not so high that food sticks and burns.

5 Foods should be added in a specific order, usually aromatics first (garlic, ginger, spring onions), followed by the main ingredients which require some cooking, such as meats and denser vegetables and then the finer ingredients. Keep the ingredients moving in the pan with a long-handled spatula or wooden spoon. If the ingredients in the wok begin to dry out, add a splash of water.

COOK'S TIP
The advantage of cooking with a wok is that its gently sloping sides allow the heat to spread rapidly and evenly over the surface, enabling food to cook quickly, retaining flavour, colour and nutrients.

Pork Satay with Crispy Noodle Cake

Crispy noodles are a popular and tasty accompaniment to satay, and are particularly good with the spicy satay sauce.

Serves 4–6

INGREDIENTS
450 g/1 lb lean pork
3 garlic cloves, finely chopped
15 ml/1 tbsp Thai curry powder
5 ml/1 tsp ground cumin
5 ml/1 tsp sugar
15 ml/1 tbsp fish sauce
90 ml/6 tbsp oil
350 g/12 oz thin egg noodles
fresh coriander, to garnish

FOR THE SATAY SAUCE
30 ml/2 tbsp oil
2 garlic cloves, finely chopped
1 small onion, finely chopped
2.5 ml/½ tsp hot chilli powder
5 ml/1 tsp Thai curry powder
250 ml/8 fl oz/1 cup coconut milk
15 ml/1 tbsp fish sauce
30 ml/2 tbsp sugar
juice of ½ lemon
165 g/5½ oz crunchy peanut butter

1 Cut the pork into thin 5-cm/2-in-long strips. Mix the garlic, curry powder, cumin, sugar and fish sauce in a bowl. Stir in about 30 ml/2 tbsp of the oil. Add the meat to the bowl, toss to coat and leave to marinate in a cool place for at least 2 hours. Meanwhile cook the noodles in a large saucepan of boiling water until just tender. Drain thoroughly.

2 Make the satay sauce. Heat the oil in a saucepan and fry the garlic and onion with the chilli powder and curry powder for 2–3 minutes. Stir in the coconut milk, fish sauce, sugar, lemon juice and peanut butter. Mix well. Reduce the heat and cook, stirring frequently, for about 20 minutes or until the sauce thickens. Be careful not to let the sauce stick to the bottom of the pan or it will burn.

pork *garlic* *onion* *Thai curry powder* *ground cumin* *sugar* *fish sauce* *egg noodles* *fresh coriander* *hot chilli powder* *coconut milk* *lemon* *crunchy peanut butter*

3 Heat about 15 ml/1 tbsp of the remaining oil in a frying pan. Spread the noodles evenly over the pan and fry for 4–5 minutes until crisp and golden. Turn the noodle cake over carefully and cook the other side until crisp. Keep hot.

4 Drain the meat and thread it on to the drained skewers. Cook under a hot grill for 8–10 minutes until cooked, turning occasionally and brushing with the remaining oil. Serve with wedges of noodle cake, accompanied by the satay sauce. Garnish with coriander leaves.

Vegetable Spring Rolls with Sweet Chilli Sauce

Vermicelli noodles need hardly any cooking before stirring into the tasty vegetable filling.

Makes 20–24

INGREDIENTS

25 g/1 oz rice vermicelli noodles
oil, for deep-frying
5 ml/1 tsp grated fresh root ginger
2 spring onions, finely shredded
50 g/2 oz carrot, finely grated
50 g/2 oz mangetouts, thinly sliced
25 g/1 oz young spinach leaves
50 g/2 oz/¼ cup beansprouts
15 ml/1 tbsp chopped fresh mint
15 ml/1 tbsp chopped fresh
    coriander
30 ml/2 tbsp fish sauce
20–24 spring roll wrappers,
    each 13 cm/5 in square
1 egg white, lightly beaten

FOR THE DIPPING SAUCE

50 g/2 oz/4 tbsp caster sugar
50 ml/3½ tbsp rice vinegar
2 red chillies, seeded and finely
    chopped

rice vermicelli noodles

spring onions

mangetouts

fresh coriander

beansprouts

fish sauce

spring roll wrappers

red chillies

1 First make the dipping sauce: place the sugar and vinegar in a small pan with 30 ml/2 tbsp water. Heat gently, stirring until the sugar dissolves, then boil rapidly until it forms a light syrup. Stir in the chillies and leave to cool.

2 Soak the noodles according to the packet instructions; rinse and drain well. Using scissors, snip the noodles into short lengths.

3 Heat 15 ml/1 tbsp of the oil in a wok and stir-fry the ginger and spring onions for 15 seconds. Add the carrot and mangetouts and stir-fry for 2–3 minutes. Add the spinach, beansprouts, mint, coriander, fish sauce and noodles and stir-fry for a further minute. Set aside.

4 Take one spring roll wrapper and arrange it so that it faces you in a diamond shape. Place a spoonful of filling just below the centre, then fold up the bottom point over the filling.

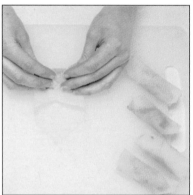

5 Fold in each side, then roll up tightly. Brush the end with beaten egg white to seal. Repeat this process until all the filling has been used.

6 Half-fill a wok with oil and heat to 180°C/350°F. Deep-fry the spring rolls in batches for 3–4 minutes until golden. Drain. Serve hot with the chilli sauce.

COOK'S TIP

Use groundnut oil for this recipe or otherwise sunflower oil. Groundnut oil has a distinct flavour and gives an authentic taste. Sunflower oil is milder but still very good.

Japanese Chilled Noodles with Dashi Dip

This classic Japanese dish of cold noodles is known as *somen*. The noodles are surprisingly refreshing when eaten with fish or fried meats and the delicately flavoured dip.

Serves 4–6

INGREDIENTS
15–30 ml/1–2 tbsp oil
2 medium eggs, beaten with a pinch
   of salt
1 sheet yaki-nori seaweed, finely
   shredded
½ bunch spring onions, thinly sliced
wasabi paste
400 g/14 oz dried somen noodles
ice cubes, for serving

FOR THE DIP
1 litre/1¾ pints/4 cups kombu and
   bonito stock or instant dashi
200 ml/7 fl oz/scant 1 cup Japanese
   soy sauce
15 ml/1 tbsp mirin

eggs

spring onions

wasabi paste

mirin

kombu and bonito stock

soy sauce

dried somen noodles

1 Prepare the dashi dip in advance so that it has time to cool and chill. Using either kombu and bonito stock or instant dashi, bring all the ingredients to the boil. Leave to cool and chill thoroughly.

   Meanwhile, heat a little oil in a frying pan. Pour in half the beaten eggs, tilting the pan to coat the base evenly. Leave to set, then turn the omelette over and cook the second side briefly. Turn out on to a board. Cook the remaining egg in the same way.

2 Leave the omelettes to cool and then shred them finely. Place the shredded omelette, yaki nori, spring onions and wasabi in four small bowls.

3 Boil the somen noodles according to the packet instructions and drain. Rinse the noodles thoroughly under cold, running water, stirring with chopsticks, then drain thoroughly again.

4 Place the noodles on a large plate and add some ice cubes on top to keep them cool. Pour the cold dip into four small bowls. Noodles and accompaniments are dipped into the chilled dip before they are eaten.

Chinese-style Cabbage and Noodle Parcels

The noodles and Chinese mushrooms give a delightful oriental flavour to these traditional cabbage rolls. Serve with rice for a tasty meal.

Serves 4–6

INGREDIENTS
4 dried Chinese mushrooms, soaked
    in hot water until soft
50 g/2 oz cellophane noodles,
    soaked in hot water until soft
450 g/1 lb minced pork
2 garlic cloves, finely chopped
8 spring onions
30 ml/2 tbsp fish sauce
12 large outer green cabbage leaves

FOR THE SAUCE
30 ml/2 tbsp oil
1 small onion, finely chopped
2 garlic cloves, crushed
400 g/14 oz can chopped plum
    tomatoes
pinch of sugar
salt and freshly ground black pepper

Chinese mushrooms   *spring onions*

cellophane noodles   *minced pork*

garlic   *fish sauce*   *onion*

chopped plum tomatoes

1 Drain the mushrooms, discard the stems and chop the caps. Put them in a bowl. Next, drain the noodles and cut them into short lengths. Add to the bowl with the pork and garlic. Chop two of the spring onions and add to the bowl. Season with the fish sauce and pepper.

2 Blanch the cabbage leaves a few at a time in a saucepan of boiling, salted water for about 1 minute. Remove the leaves from the pan and refresh under cold water. Drain and dry on kitchen paper. Blanch the remaining six spring onions in the same fashion. Drain well. Fill one of the cabbage leaves with a generous spoonful of the pork and noodle filling. Taking hold of the corner closest to yourself, roll up the leaf sufficiently to enclose the filling, then tuck in the sides and continue rolling the leaf to make a tight parcel. Make more parcels in the same way.

5 Season the tomato mixture with salt, pepper and a pinch of sugar, then bring to simmering point. Add the cabbage parcels. Cover and cook gently for 20–25 minutes or until the filling is cooked. Taste the sauce to check the seasoning and serve at once.

3 Split each spring onion lengthways by cutting through the bulb and then tearing upwards. Tie each of the cabbage parcels with a length of spring onion.

4 To make the sauce, heat the oil in a large frying pan and add the onion and garlic. Fry for 2 minutes until soft. Tip the plum tomatoes into a bowl. Mash with a fork then add to the onion mixture.

COOK'S TIP

If at any time the tomato sauce looks a little dry, add some water or vegetable stock to the pan and stir through.

Thai Pork Spring Rolls

Crunchy spring rolls are as popular in Thai cuisine as they are in Chinese. In this version they are filled with noodles, garlic and pork.

Makes about 24

INGREDIENTS
4–6 dried Chinese mushrooms, soaked in hot water until soft
50 g/2 oz cellophane noodles
30 ml/2 tbsp oil
2 garlic cloves, chopped
2 red chillies, seeded and chopped
225 g/8 oz minced pork
50 g/2 oz cooked peeled prawns, chopped
30 ml/2 tbsp fish sauce
5 ml/1 tsp sugar
freshly ground black pepper
1 carrot, very finely sliced
50 g/2 oz bamboo shoots, chopped
50 g/2 oz/¼ cup beansprouts
2 spring onions, chopped
15 ml/1 tbsp chopped fresh coriander
30 ml/2 tbsp plain flour
24 x 15 cm/6 in square spring roll wrappers
oil, for deep-frying
Thai sweet chilli sauce, to serve (optional)

Chinese mushrooms

cellophane noodles

garlic

minced pork

cooked prawns

fish sauce

beansprouts

fresh coriander

spring roll wrappers

1 Drain and finely chop the Chinese mushrooms. Remove and discard the stems. Soak the noodles in hot water until soft, then drain. Cut into short lengths, about 5 cm/2 in.

2 Heat the oil in a wok or large frying pan, add the garlic and chillies and fry for 30 seconds. Add the pork and stir-fry for a few minutes until the meat is browned. Add the noodles, mushrooms and prawns. Season with fish sauce, sugar and pepper. Tip into a bowl. Add the carrot, bamboo shoots, beansprouts, spring onions and coriander and stir well to mix.

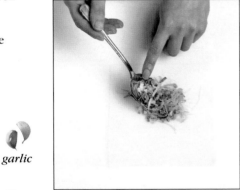

3 Put the flour in a small bowl and blend with a little water to make a paste. Place a spoonful of filling in the centre of a spring roll wrapper.

4 Turn the bottom edge over to cover the filling, then fold in the left and right sides. Roll the wrapper up almost to the top edge. Brush the top edge with flour paste and seal. Repeat with the rest of the wrappers.

5 Heat the oil in a wok or deep-fat fryer. Slide in the spring rolls a few at a time and fry until crisp and golden brown. Remove with a slotted spoon and drain on kitchen paper. Serve with Thai sweet chilli sauce to dip them into, if liked.

Fried Monkfish Coated with Rice Noodles

These marinated medallions of fish are coated in rice vermicelli and deep-fried – they taste as good as they look.

Serves 4

INGREDIENTS
450 g/1 lb monkfish
5 ml/1 tsp grated fresh root ginger
1 garlic clove, finely chopped
30 ml/2 tbsp light soy sauce
175 g/6 oz rice vermicelli noodles
50 g/2 oz cornflour
2 eggs, beaten
oil, for deep-frying
banana leaves, to serve (optional)

FOR THE DIPPING SAUCE
30 ml/2 tbsp light soy sauce
30 ml/2 tbsp rice vinegar
15 ml/1 tbsp sugar
salt and freshly ground black pepper
2 red chillies, seeded and thinly sliced
1 spring onion, thinly sliced

monkfish

fresh root ginger

garlic

light soy sauce

rice vermicelli noodles

eggs

rice vinegar

sugar

red chillies

spring onion

1 Cut the monkfish into 2.5-cm/1-in-thick medallions. Place in a dish and add the ginger, garlic and soy sauce. Leave to marinate for 10 minutes. For the dipping sauce, heat the soy sauce, vinegar and sugar in a saucepan until boiling. Add the salt and pepper. Remove from the heat, add the chillies and spring onion.

2 Using kitchen scissors, cut the noodles into 4-cm/1½-in lengths. Spread them out in a shallow bowl.

3 Coat the fish medallions in cornflour, dip in beaten egg and cover with noodles, pressing them on to the fish so that they stick.

4 Deep-fry the coated fish in hot oil, 2–3 pieces at a time, until the noodle coating is crisp and golden brown. Drain and serve hot on banana leaves if you like, accompanied by the dipping sauce.

Deep-fried Wonton Cushions with Sambal Kecap

These delicious, golden packages, called *pansit goreng*, are popular in Indonesia as party fare or for a quick snack.

Makes 40

INGREDIENTS
115 g/4 oz pork fillet, trimmed and
   sliced
225 g/8 oz cooked peeled prawns
2–3 garlic cloves, crushed
2 spring onions, roughly chopped
15 ml/1 tbsp cornflour
about 40 wonton wrappers
oil, for deep-frying
salt and freshly ground black pepper

FOR THE SAMBAL KECAP
1–2 red chillies, seeded and sliced
1–2 garlic cloves, crushed
45 ml/3 tbsp dark soy sauce
45–60 ml/3–4 tbsp lemon or
   lime juice

cornflour

pork fillet

cooked prawns

garlic

spring onions

wonton wrappers

red chillies

lemon juice

dark soy sauce

1 Grind the slices of pork finely in a food processor. Add the prawns, garlic, spring onions and cornflour. Season to taste and then process briefly.

2 Place a little of the prepared filling on to each wonton wrapper, just off centre, with the wrapper positioned like a diamond in front of you. Dampen all the edges, except for the uppermost corner of the diamond.

3 Lift the corner nearest to you towards the filling and then roll up the wrapper, to cover the filling. Turn over. Bring the two extreme corners together, sealing one on top of the other. Squeeze lightly, to plump up the filling. Repeat the process until all the wrappers and the filling are used up. The prepared 'cushions' and any leftover wonton wrappers can be frozen at this stage.

4 Meanwhile, prepare the sambal. Mix the chillies and garlic together and then stir in the dark soy sauce, lemon or lime juice and 15–30 ml/1–2 tbsp water. Pour into a serving bowl and set aside.

5 Deep-fry the wonton cushions in hot oil, a few at a time, for about 2–3 minutes, or until cooked through, crisp and golden brown. Serve on a large platter together with the sambal kecap.

Alfalfa Crab Salad with Crispy Fried Noodles

The crispy noodles make a delicious contrast, both in flavour and texture, with this healthy mixture of crab and vegetables.

Serves 4–6

INGREDIENTS
oil, for deep-frying
50 g/2 oz Chinese rice noodles
150 g/5 oz frozen white crab meat, thawed
115 g/4 oz/½ cup alfalfa sprouts
1 small iceberg lettuce
4 sprigs fresh coriander, roughly chopped
1 ripe tomato, skinned, seeded and diced
4 sprigs fresh mint, roughly chopped, plus an extra sprig to garnish

FOR THE SESAME LIME DRESSING
45 ml/3 tbsp vegetable oil
5 ml/1 tsp sesame oil
½ small red chilli, seeded and finely chopped
1 piece stem ginger in syrup, cut into matchsticks
10 ml/2 tsp stem ginger syrup
10 ml/2 tsp light soy sauce
juice of ½ lime

Chinese rice noodles

crab meat

alfalfa sprouts

iceberg lettuce

tomato

mint

fresh coriander

red chilli

lime juice

1 First make the dressing: combine the vegetable and sesame oils in a bowl. Add the chilli, stem ginger, stem ginger syrup and soy sauce and stir in the lime juice. Set aside.

2 Heat the oil in a wok or deep-fat fryer to 196°C/385°F. Fry the noodles, one handful at a time, until crisp. Lift out and drain on kitchen paper.

3 Flake the white crab meat into a bowl and toss with the alfalfa sprouts.

4 Finely chop the lettuce and mix with the coriander, tomato and mint. Place in a bowl, top with the noodles and the crab meat and alfalfa salad and garnish with a sprig of mint. Serve with the sesame lime dressing.

Smoked Trout and Noodle Salad

This salad is a wonderful example of how well noodles can combine with Mediterranean ingredients, such as trout, capers and tomato.

Serves 4

INGREDIENTS
225 g/8 oz somen noodles
2 smoked trout, skinned and boned
2 hard-boiled eggs, coarsely chopped
30 ml/2 tbsp snipped chives
lime halves, to serve (optional)

FOR THE DRESSING
6 ripe plum tomatoes
2 shallots, finely chopped
30 ml/2 tbsp tiny capers, rinsed
30 ml/2 tbsp chopped fresh tarragon
finely grated rind and juice of ½ orange
60 ml/4 tbsp extra-virgin olive oil
salt and freshly ground black pepper

somen noodles

smoked trout

chives

hard-boiled eggs

olive oil

orange juice and grated rind

plum tomatoes

shallots

fresh tarragon

1 To make the dressing, cut the tomatoes in half, remove the cores and cut the flesh into chunks. Place in a bowl with the shallots, capers, tarragon, orange rind, orange juice and olive oil. Season with salt and pepper, and mix well. Leave the dressing to marinate for 1–2 hours.

2 Cook the noodles in a large saucepan of boiling water until just tender. Drain and rinse under cold, running water. Drain well.

COOK'S TIP
Choose tomatoes that are firm, bright in colour and have a matt texture, avoiding any with blotched or cracked skins.

3 Toss the noodles with the dressing, then adjust the seasoning to taste. Arrange the noodles on a large serving platter or individual plates.

4 Flake the smoked trout over the noodles, then sprinkle the coarsely chopped eggs and snipped chives over the top. Serve the lime halves on the side, if you like.

Beef Noodle Soup

This rich, satisfying soup is packed with all sorts of flavours and textures, brought together with delicious egg noodles.

Serves 4

INGREDIENTS

10 g/¼ oz dried porcini mushrooms
6 spring onions
115 g/4 oz carrots
350 g/12 oz rump steak
about 30 ml/2 tbsp oil
1 garlic clove, crushed
2.5 cm/1 in fresh root ginger,
   finely chopped
1.2 litres/2 pints/5 cups beef stock
45 ml/3 tbsp light soy sauce
60 ml/4 tbsp dry sherry
75 g/3 oz thin egg noodles
75 g/3 oz spinach, shredded
salt and freshly ground black pepper

dried porcini mushrooms   *spring onions*

carrots   *rump steak*

garlic

fresh root ginger   *beef stock*   *dry sherry*

light soy sauce

egg noodles   *spinach*

1 Break the mushrooms into small pieces, place in a bowl and pour over 150 ml/¼ pint/⅔ cup boiling water. Leave to soak for 15 minutes.

2 Cut the spring onions and carrots into 5-cm/2-in-long, fine strips. Trim any fat off the meat and slice into thin strips.

3 Heat the oil in a large saucepan and cook the beef in batches until browned, adding a little more oil if necessary. Remove the beef with a slotted spoon and drain on kitchen paper.

4 Add the garlic, ginger, spring onions and carrots to the pan and stir-fry for 3 minutes.

5 Add the beef stock, the mushrooms and their soaking liquid, the soy sauce, sherry and plenty of seasoning. Bring to the boil and simmer, covered, for 10 minutes.

6 Break up the noodles slightly and add to the pan, with the spinach. Simmer gently for 5 minutes, or until the beef is tender. Adjust the seasoning before serving.

Chiang Mai Noodle Soup

A signature dish of the Thai city of Chiang Mai, this richly flavoured and aromatic noodle soup has Burmese origins.

Serves 4–6

INGREDIENTS

600 ml/1 pint/2½ cups coconut milk
30 ml/2 tbsp red curry paste
5 ml/1 tsp ground turmeric
450 g/1 lb chicken thighs, boned
    and cut into bite-size chunks
600 ml/1 pint/2½ cups chicken stock
60 ml/4 tbsp fish sauce
15 ml/1 tbsp dark soy sauce
juice of ½–1 lime
450 g/1 lb fresh egg noodles,
    blanched briefly in boiling water
salt and freshly ground black pepper

FOR THE GARNISH

3 spring onions, chopped
4 red chillies
4 shallots, chopped
60 ml/4 tbsp sliced pickled mustard
    leaves, rinsed
30 ml/2 tbsp fried sliced garlic
fresh coriander sprigs

coconut milk

red curry paste

ground turmeric

chicken stock

chicken thighs

fish sauce

dark soy sauce

lime

fresh egg noodles

red chillies

spring onions

fresh coriander

1 Pour about one third of the coconut milk into a saucepan and bring to the boil, stirring frequently until it separates.

2 Add the curry paste and ground turmeric, stir to mix completely and cook for a few minutes, until blended.

3 Add the chicken pieces to the saucepan and stir-fry for about 2 minutes. Ensure that all the chunks of meat are coated with the paste.

4 Add the remaining coconut milk, stock, fish sauce, soy sauce and seasoning. Simmer for 7–10 minutes. Remove from the heat and add the lime juice.

Reheat the noodles in boiling water, then drain. Divide the noodles and chicken among the bowls and ladle over the hot soup. Top with the garnishes.

Pork and Pickled Mustard Greens Soup

The pickled mustard leaves give the flavour while the cellophane noodles bring texture to this traditional Thai soup.

Serves 4–6

INGREDIENTS

225 g/8 oz pickled mustard leaves, soaked
50 g/2 oz cellophane noodles, soaked
15 ml/1 tbsp oil
4 garlic cloves, finely sliced
1 litre/1¾ pints/4 cups chicken stock
450 g/1 lb pork ribs, cut into large chunks
30 ml/2 tbsp fish sauce
pinch of sugar
freshly ground black pepper
2 red chillies, seeded and finely sliced, to garnish

cellophane noodles

garlic

chicken stock

fish sauce

pork ribs

red chillies

1 Drain the pickled mustard leaves and cut them into bite-size pieces. Taste to check the seasoning is to your liking. If they are too salty, soak them in water for a little bit longer.

2 Drain the cellophane noodles and cut them into short lengths.

3 Heat the oil in a small frying pan, add the garlic and stir-fry until golden, taking care not to let it burn. Transfer the mixture to a bowl and set aside.

4 Put the stock in a saucepan, bring to the boil, then add the pork and simmer gently for 10–15 minutes. Add the pickled mustard leaves and cellophane noodles. Bring back to the boil. Season to taste with fish sauce, sugar and freshly ground black pepper. Serve hot, topped with the fried garlic and red chillies.

Hanoi Beef and Noodle Soup

Millions of North Vietnamese eat this fragrant noodle soup every day for breakfast.

Serves 4–6

INGREDIENTS
1 onion
1.5 kg/3–3½ lb stewing beef
2.5 cm/1 in fresh root ginger, peeled
1 star anise
1 bay leaf
2 whole cloves
2.5 ml/½ tsp fennel seeds
1 piece cassia or cinnamon stick
fish sauce, to taste
juice of 1 lime
150 g/5 oz fillet steak
450 g/1 lb fresh flat rice noodles
salt and freshly ground black pepper
handful of fresh coriander leaves
    and lime wedges, to garnish

FOR THE ACCOMPANIMENTS
1 small red onion, sliced into rings
115 g/4 oz/½ cup beansprouts
2 red chillies, seeded and sliced
2 spring onions, finely sliced

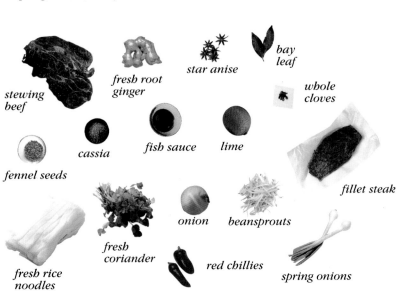

stewing beef · fresh root ginger · star anise · bay leaf · whole cloves · cassia · fish sauce · lime · fennel seeds · fillet steak · fresh coriander · onion · beansprouts · red chillies · spring onions · fresh rice noodles

1 Cut the onion in half. Grill under a high heat, cut side up, until the exposed sides are caramelized and deep brown.

2 Cut the stewing beef into large chunks and then place in a large saucepan or stock pot. Add the caramelized onion with the ginger, star anise, bay leaf, cloves, fennel seeds and cassia or cinnamon stick.

3 Add 3 litres/5 pints/12½ cups water, bring to the boil, reduce the heat and simmer gently for 2–3 hours, skimming off the fat and scum from time to time.

4 Using a slotted spoon, remove the meat from the stock; when cool enough to handle, cut into small pieces. Strain the stock and return to the pan or stock pot together with the meat. Bring back to the boil and season with the fish sauce, lime juice and salt and pepper to taste.

5 Slice the fillet steak very thinly and then chill until required. Cook the noodles in a large pan of boiling water until just tender. Drain and divide among individual serving bowls. Arrange the thinly sliced steak over the noodles, pour the hot stock on top and garnish with coriander and lime wedges. Serve, offering the accompaniments in separate bowls.

Malaysian Spicy Prawn and Noodle Soup

This is a Malaysian version of Hanoi Beef and Noodle Soup using fish and prawns instead of beef. If laksa noodles aren't available, flat rice noodles can be used instead.

Serves 4–6

COOK'S TIP

To serve, line a serving platter with the lettuce leaves. Arrange all the ingredients, including the bean-sprouts, spring onions, cucumber and prawn crackers, in neat piles. Serve the soup from a large tureen or stoneware pot.

INGREDIENTS

25 g/1 oz unsalted cashew nuts
3 shallots, or 1 medium onion, sliced
5 cm/2 in lemon grass, shredded
2 cloves garlic, crushed
30 ml/2 tbsp oil
1 cm/½ in cube shrimp paste or 15 ml/1 tbsp fish sauce
15 ml/1 tbsp mild curry paste
400 ml/14 fl oz/1⅔ cups coconut milk
½ chicken stock cube
3 curry leaves (optional)
450 g/1 lb white fish fillets, e.g. cod, haddock or whiting
225 g/8 oz prawns, fresh or cooked
150 g/5 oz laksa noodles, soaked for 10 minutes before cooking
1 small cos lettuce, shredded
115 g/4 oz/½ cup beansprouts
3 spring onions, cut into lengths
½ cucumber, thinly sliced
prawn crackers, to serve

1 Grind the cashew nuts using a pestle and mortar and then spoon into a food processor and process with the shallots or onion, lemon grass and garlic.

2 Heat the oil in a large wok or saucepan, add the cashew and onion mixture, and fry for about 1–2 minutes, until the mixture begins to brown.

3 Add the shrimp paste or fish sauce and curry paste, followed by the coconut milk, stock cube and curry leaves, if using. Simmer for 10 minutes.

cashew nuts (unsalted)

garlic   *shrimp paste*

curry paste

curry leaves

coconut milk   *white fish fillets*   *prawns*

laksa noodles

lemon grass   *beansprouts*   *cucumber*

shallots   *spring onions*

4 Cut the white fish into bite-size pieces. Add the fish and prawns in the coconut stock, immersing them with a frying basket or a slotted spoon. Cook for 3–4 minutes until the fish is tender. Cook the noodles according to the instructions on the packet.

Cheat's Shark's Fin Soup

Shark's fin soup is a renowned delicacy. In this vegetarian version cellophane noodles mimic shark's fin needles.

Serves 4–6

INGREDIENTS
4 dried Chinese mushrooms
25 ml/1½ tbsp dried wood ears
115 g/4 oz cellophane noodles
30 ml/2 tbsp oil
2 carrots, cut into fine strips
115 g/4 oz canned bamboo shoots,
    rinsed, drained and cut into
    fine strips
1 litre/1¾ pints/4 cups vegetable
    stock
15 ml/1 tbsp light soy sauce
15 ml/1 tbsp arrowroot or
    potato flour
1 egg white, beaten (optional)
5 ml/1 tsp sesame oil
salt and freshly ground black pepper
2 spring onions, finely chopped, to
    garnish
Chinese red vinegar, to serve
    (optional)

dried Chinese mushrooms

dried wood ears

cellophane noodles

carrots

bamboo shoots

vegetable stock

light soy sauce

egg

sesame oil

spring onions

1 Soak the mushrooms and wood ears separately in warm water for 20 minutes. Drain. Remove the mushroom stems and slice the caps thinly. Cut the wood ears into fine strips, discarding any hard bits. Soak the noodles in hot water until soft. Drain and cut into short lengths.

2 Heat the oil in a large saucepan. Add the mushrooms and stir-fry for 2 minutes. Add the wood ears, stir-fry for 2 minutes, then stir in the carrots, bamboo shoots and noodles.

3 Add the stock to the pan. Bring to the boil, then simmer for 15–20 minutes.

4 Season with salt, pepper and soy sauce. Blend the arrowroot or potato flour with about 30 ml/2 tbsp water. Pour into the soup, stirring all the time to prevent lumps from forming as the soup continues to simmer.

5 Remove the pan from the heat. Stir in the egg white, if using, so that it sets to form small threads in the hot soup. Stir in the sesame oil, then pour the soup into individual bowls. Sprinkle each portion with chopped spring onions and offer the Chinese red vinegar separately, if using.

Noodles, Chicken and Prawns in Coconut Broth

This dish takes a well-flavoured broth and adds noodles and a delicious combination of other ingredients to make a satisfying main course.

Serves 8

INGREDIENTS
2 onions, quartered
2.5 cm/1 in fresh root ginger, sliced
2 garlic cloves
4 macadamia nuts or 8 almonds
1–2 chillies, seeded and sliced
2 lemon grass stems, lower
    5 cm/2 in sliced
5 cm/2 in fresh turmeric, peeled and
    sliced, or 5 ml/1 tsp ground
    turmeric
15 ml/1 tbsp coriander seeds,
    dry-fried
5 ml/1 tsp cumin seeds, dry-fried
60 ml/4 tbsp oil
400 ml/14 fl oz/1⅔ cups coconut
    milk
1.5 litres/2½ pints/6¼ cups chicken
    stock
375 g/13 oz rice noodles, soaked in
    cold water
350 g/12 oz cooked tiger prawns
salt and freshly ground black pepper

FOR THE GARNISH
4 hard-boiled eggs, quartered
225 g/8 oz cooked chicken, chopped
225 g/8 oz/1 cup beansprouts
1 bunch spring onions, shredded
deep-fried onions (optional)

lemon grass

fresh turmeric

coriander seeds

coconut milk

chicken

rice noodles

tiger prawns

eggs

beansprouts

spring onions

1 Place the quartered onions, ginger, garlic and nuts in a food processor with the chillies, sliced lemon grass and turmeric. Process to a paste. Alternatively, pound all the ingredients with a pestle and mortar. Grind the coriander and cumin seeds coarsely and add to the paste.

2 Heat the oil in a pan and fry the spice paste, without colouring, to bring out the flavours. Add the coconut milk, stock and seasoning and simmer for 5–10 minutes.

3 Meanwhile, drain the rice noodles and plunge them into a large pan of salted, boiling water for 2 minutes. Remove from the heat and drain well. Rinse thoroughly with plenty of cold water, to halt the cooking process.

4 Add the tiger prawns to the soup just before serving and heat through for a minute or two. Arrange the garnishes in separate bowls. Each person helps themselves to noodles, adds soup, eggs, chicken and beansprouts and then scatters shredded spring onions and deep-fried onions, if liked, on top.

COOK'S TIP

To dry-fry spices, heat a small heavy-based pan over a medium heat for 1 minute, add the spices and cook for 2–3 minutes, stirring frequently. Remove from the heat and grind the spices using a mortar and pestle.

Beef Soup with Noodles and Meatballs

Egg noodles and spicy meatballs make this a really sustaining main meal soup. In the east it is often served from street stalls.

Serves 6

INGREDIENTS

450 g/1 lb dried medium egg
    noodles
45 ml/3 tbsp sunflower oil
1 large onion, finely sliced
2 garlic cloves, crushed
2.5 cm/1 in fresh root ginger, cut
    into thin matchsticks
1.2 litres/2 pints/5 cups beef stock
30 ml/2 tbsp dark soy sauce
2 celery sticks, finely sliced, leaves
    reserved
6 Chinese leaves, cut into bite-size
    pieces
1 handful mangetouts, cut
    into strips
salt and freshly ground black pepper

FOR THE MEATBALLS

1 large onion, roughly chopped
1–2 red chillies, seeded and
    chopped
2 garlic cloves, crushed
1 cm/½ in cube shrimp paste
450 g/1 lb lean minced beef
15 ml/1 tbsp ground coriander
5 ml/1 tsp ground cumin
10 ml/2 tsp dark soy sauce
5 ml/1 tsp dark brown sugar
juice of ½ lemon
a little beaten egg

dark soy sauce   dark brown sugar   lemon juice   mangetouts   Chinese leaves

egg   celery   fresh root ginger   dried egg noodles   beef stock

red chillies   garlic   ground coriander   ground cumin   minced beef   onion

1 For the meatballs, put the onion, chillies, garlic and shrimp paste in a food processor. Process in short bursts, taking care not to over-chop the onion.

2 Put the meat in a large bowl. Stir in the onion mixture. Add the ground coriander and cumin, soy sauce, sugar, lemon juice and seasoning.

COOK'S TIP

COOK'S TIP

Shrimp paste, or *terasi*, has a strong, salty, distinctive flavour and smell. Use sparingly if unsure of its flavour.

3 Bind the mixture with a little beaten egg and shape into small balls.

4 Cook the noodles in a large pan of boiling, salted water for 3–4 minutes, or until *al dente*. Drain in a colander and rinse with plenty of cold water. Set aside. Heat the oil in a wide pan and fry the onion, garlic and ginger until soft but not browned. Add the stock and soy sauce and bring to the boil.

5 Add the meatballs, half-cover and simmer until they are cooked, about 5–8 minutes. Just before serving, add the sliced celery and, after 2 minutes, the Chinese leaves and mangetouts. Adjust the seasoning. Divide the noodles among soup bowls, pour the soup on top and garnish with the reserved celery leaves.

Japanese Noodle Casseroles

Traditionally these individual casseroles are cooked in earthenware pots. *Nabe* means "pot" and *yaki* means "to heat", providing the Japanese title of *nabeyaki udon* for this recipe.

Serves 4

INGREDIENTS

115 g/4 oz boneless chicken thighs
2.5 ml/½ tsp salt
2.5 ml/½ tsp sake or dry white wine
2.5 ml/½ tsp light soy sauce
1 leek
115 g/4 oz fresh spinach, trimmed
300 g/11 oz dried udon noodles or
    500 g/1¼ lb fresh udon noodles
4 shiitake mushrooms, stems
    removed
4 medium eggs
shichimi or seven-flavour spice, to
    serve (optional)

FOR THE SOUP

1.4 litres/2⅓ pints/6 cups kombu and
    bonito stock or instant dashi
25 ml/1½ tbsp light soy sauce
5 ml/1 tsp salt
15 ml/1 tbsp mirin

chicken thighs
light soy sauce
leek
sake
spinach
shiitake mushrooms
udon noodles
eggs
kombu and bonito stock
mirin

1 Cut the chicken into small chunks and sprinkle with the salt, sake or wine and soy sauce. Cut the leek diagonally into 4-cm/1½-in slices.

3 For the soup, bring the kombu and bonito stock, soy sauce, salt and mirin to the boil in a saucepan and add the chicken and leek. Skim the broth, then simmer for 5 minutes.

2 Boil the spinach for 1–2 minutes, then drain and soak in cold water for 1 minute. Drain, squeeze lightly, then cut into 4-cm/1½-in lengths. If using dried udon noodles, boil them according to the packet instructions, allowing 3 minutes less than the stated cooking time. Place fresh udon noodles in boiling water, disentangle, then drain.

4 Divide the udon noodles among four individual flameproof casseroles. Pour the soup, chicken and leeks into the casseroles. Place over a moderate heat and add the shiitake mushrooms. Gently break an egg into each casserole. Cover and simmer gently for 2 minutes.

5 Divide the spinach among the casseroles and simmer, covered, for a further 1 minute.

6 Serve immediately, standing the hot casseroles on plates or table mats. Sprinkle seven-flavour spice over the casseroles if liked.

COOK'S TIP

Assorted tempura using vegetables, such as sweet potato, carrot and shiitake mushrooms, and fish such as squid and prawns could be served in these casseroles instead of chicken and egg.

Crispy Noodles with Mixed Vegetables

In this dish, rice vermicelli noodles are deep-fried until crisp, then tossed into a colourful selection of stir-fried vegetables.

Serves 3–4

INGREDIENTS
2 large carrots
2 courgettes
4 spring onions
115 g/4 oz yard-long beans or
    green beans
115 g/4 oz dried rice vermicelli or
    cellophane noodles
oil, for deep-frying
2.5 cm/1 in fresh root ginger, cut
    into shreds
1 red chilli, seeded and sliced
115 g/4 oz fresh shiitake or button
    mushrooms, thickly sliced
a few Chinese cabbage leaves,
    coarsely shredded
75 g/3 oz/⅓ cup beansprouts
30 ml/2 tbsp light soy sauce
30 ml/2 tbsp Chinese rice wine
5 ml/1 tsp sugar
30 ml/2 tbsp roughly torn coriander
    leaves

carrots
spring onions
yard-long beans
dried rice vermicelli noodles
fresh root ginger
red chillies
Chinese cabbage
beansprouts
shiitake mushrooms
light soy sauce
courgettes
Chinese rice wine
fresh coriander

1 Cut the carrots and courgettes into fine sticks. Shred the spring onions into similar-size pieces. Trim the beans. If using yard-long beans, cut them into short lengths.

2 Break the noodles into lengths of about 7.5 cm/3 in. Half-fill a wok with oil and heat it to 180°C/350°F. Deep-fry the raw noodles, a handful at a time, for 1–2 minutes, until puffed and crispy. Drain on kitchen paper. Carefully pour off all but 30 ml/2 tbsp of the oil.

4 Add the Chinese cabbage, beansprouts and spring onions. Stir-fry for 1 minute, then add the soy sauce, rice wine and sugar. Cook, stirring, for about 30 seconds.

COOK'S TIP
If a milder flavour is preferred, remove the seeds from the chilli.

3 Reheat the oil in the wok. When hot, add the beans and stir-fry for 2–3 minutes. Add the ginger, red chilli, mushrooms, carrots and courgettes and stir-fry for 1–2 minutes.

5 Add the noodles and coriander and toss to mix, taking care not to crush the noodles too much. Serve at once, piled up on a plate.

Chinese Mushrooms with Cellophane Noodles

Red fermented beancurd adds extra flavour to this hearty vegetarian dish. It is brick red in colour, with a very strong, cheesy flavour.

Serves 3–4

INGREDIENTS
115 g/4 oz dried Chinese
   mushrooms
25 g/1 oz dried wood ears
115 g/4 oz dried beancurd
30 ml/2 tbsp oil
2 garlic cloves, finely chopped
2 slices fresh root ginger, finely
   chopped
10 Szechuan peppercorns, crushed
15 ml/1 tbsp red fermented
   beancurd
½ star anise
pinch of sugar
15-30 ml/1–2 tbsp dark soy sauce
50 g/2 oz cellophane noodles,
   soaked in hot water until soft
salt

*dried Chinese
mushrooms*

*dried wood
ears*

*fresh root
ginger*

*Szechuan
peppercorns*

star anise

*dark soy
sauce*

*cellophane
noodles*

1 Soak the Chinese mushrooms and wood ears separately in bowls of hot water for 30 minutes. Break the dried beancurd into pieces and soak in water according to the packet instructions.

2 Strain the mushrooms, squeezing as much liquid from them as possible. Reserve the liquid. Discard the stems and cut the caps in half if they are large. Drain the wood ears, rinse and drain again. Cut off any gritty parts, then cut each wood ear into two or three pieces.

3 Heat the oil in a heavy-based pan and fry the garlic, ginger and Szechuan peppercorns for a few seconds. Add the mushrooms and red fermented beancurd, mix lightly and fry for 5 minutes.

4 Add the reserved mushroom liquid to the pan, with sufficient water to completely cover the mushrooms. Add the star anise, sugar and soy sauce, then cover and simmer for 30 seconds. Add the chopped wood ears and reconstituted beancurd pieces to the pan. Cover and cook for about 10 minutes.

5 Drain the cellophane noodles, add them to the mixture and cook for a further 10 minutes until tender, adding more liquid if necessary. Add salt to taste and serve.

Stir-fried Beancurd with Noodles

This is a satisfying dish, which is both tasty and easy to make.

Serves 4

INGREDIENTS

225 g/8 oz firm beancurd
groundnut oil, for deep-frying
175 g/6 oz medium egg noodles
15 ml/1 tbsp sesame oil
5 ml/1 tsp cornflour
10 ml/2 tsp dark soy sauce
30 ml/2 tbsp Chinese rice wine
5 ml/1 tsp sugar
6–8 spring onions, cut diagonally
    into 2.5-cm/1-in lengths
3 garlic cloves, sliced
1 green chilli, seeded and sliced
115 g/4 oz Chinese cabbage leaves,
    coarsely shredded
50 g/2 oz/¼ cup beansprouts
50 g/2 oz/½ cup cashew nuts,
    toasted

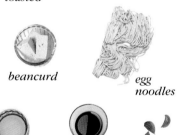

beancurd *egg noodles*

sesame oil *dark soy sauce* *garlic*

spring onions *Chinese cabbage*

green chilli *beansprouts* *cashew nuts*

1 If in water, drain the beancurd and pat dry with kitchen paper. Cut it into 2.5-cm/1-in cubes. Half-fill a wok with groundnut oil and heat to 180°C/350°F. Deep-fry the beancurd in batches for 1–2 minutes, until golden and crisp. Drain on kitchen paper. Carefully pour all but 30 ml/2 tbsp of the oil from the wok.

2 Cook the noodles. Rinse them thoroughly under cold water and drain well. Toss in 10 ml/2 tsp of the sesame oil and set aside. In a bowl, blend together the cornflour, soy sauce, rice wine, sugar and remaining sesame oil.

3 Reheat the 30 ml/2 tbsp of groundnut oil and, when hot, add the spring onions, garlic, chilli, Chinese cabbage and beansprouts. Stir-fry for 1–2 minutes.

4 Add the beancurd, noodles and cornflour sauce. Cook, stirring, for about 1 minute, until well mixed. Sprinkle over the cashew nuts. Serve at once.

Egg Noodle Stir-fry

The thick egg noodles and potatoes, along with the vegetables, make this a satisfying and healthy main dish. If possible, use fresh egg noodles, which are available from most large supermarkets.

Serves 4

INGREDIENTS

2 eggs
5 ml/1 tsp chilli powder
5 ml/1 tsp ground turmeric
60 ml/4 tbsp oil
1 large onion, finely sliced
2 red chillies, seeded and finely
    sliced
15 ml/1 tbsp light soy sauce
2 large cooked potatoes, cut into
    small cubes
6 pieces fried beancurd, sliced
225 g/8 oz/1 cup beansprouts
115 g/4 oz green beans, blanched
350 g/12 oz fresh thick egg noodles
salt and freshly ground black pepper
sliced spring onions, to garnish

eggs

chilli powder

ground turmeric

onion

red chillies

light soy sauce

potatoes

fried beancurd

bean sprouts

green beans

fresh thick egg noodles

spring onions

COOK'S TIP

Ideally wear gloves when preparing chillies; if you don't, certainly wash your hands thoroughly afterwards. Keep your hands away from your eyes as chillies will sting them.

1 Beat the eggs lightly, then strain them into a bowl. Heat a lightly greased omelette pan. Pour in half of the beaten egg to just thinly cover the bottom of the pan. When the egg is set, carefully turn the omelette over and fry the other side briefly.

2 Slide the omelette on to a plate, blot with kitchen paper, roll up and cut into narrow strips. Make a second omelette in the same way and slice. Set the omelette strips aside for the garnish.

3 In a cup, mix together the chilli powder and turmeric. Form a paste by stirring in a little water. Heat the oil in a wok or large frying pan. Fry the onion until soft. Reduce the heat and add the chilli paste, sliced chillies and soy sauce. Fry for 2–3 minutes.

4 Add the potatoes and fry for about 2 minutes, mixing well with the chillies. Add the beancurd, then the beansprouts, green beans and noodles.

5 Gently stir-fry until the noodles are evenly coated and heated through. Take care not to break up the potatoes or the beancurd. Season with salt and pepper. Serve hot, garnished with the reserved omelette strips and spring onion slices.

Peanut and Vegetable Noodles

Add any of your favourite vegetables to this recipe, which is quick to make for a great mid-week supper.

Serves 3–4

INGREDIENTS

225 g/8 oz medium egg noodles
30 ml/2 tbsp olive oil
2 garlic cloves, crushed
1 large onion, roughly chopped
1 red pepper, seeded and roughly
  chopped
1 yellow pepper, seeded and
  roughly chopped
350 g/12 oz courgettes, roughly
  chopped
150 g/5 oz/generous ½ cup roasted
  unsalted peanuts, roughly
  chopped

FOR THE DRESSING

60 ml/4 tbsp olive oil
grated rind and juice of 1 lemon
1 red chilli, seeded and finely
  chopped
45 ml/3 tbsp chopped fresh chives,
  plus extra to garnish
15–30 ml/1–2 tbsp balsamic vinegar
salt and white pepper

garlic *onion*

egg noodles *red pepper* *yellow pepper*

courgettes *peanuts* *red chilli*

chives *lemon*

1 ▮ Soak the noodles according to the packet instructions and drain well.

2 ▮ Meanwhile, heat the oil in a very large frying pan or wok and cook the garlic and onion for 3–4 minutes, until beginning to soften. Add the peppers and courgettes and cook for a further 15 minutes over a medium heat, until beginning to soften and brown. Add the peanuts and cook for a further 1 minute.

3 ▮ Make the dressing. In a bowl, whisk together the olive oil, grated lemon rind and 45 ml/3 tbsp lemon juice, the chilli, the chopped fresh chives, plenty of salt and pepper to season and balsamic vinegar to taste.

4 ▮ Toss the noodles into the vegetables and stir-fry to heat through. Add the dressing, stir to coat thoroughly and serve immediately, garnished with chopped fresh chives.

Five-spice Vegetable Noodles

Vary this vegetable stir-fry by substituting mushrooms, bamboo shoots, beansprouts, mangetouts or water chestnuts for some or all of the vegetables suggested below.

Serves 3–4

INGREDIENTS
225 g/8 oz dried thin or medium
   egg noodles
30 ml/2 tbsp sesame oil
2 carrots
1 celery stick
1 small fennel bulb
2 courgettes, halved and sliced
1 red chilli, seeded and chopped
2.5 cm/1 in fresh root ginger, grated
1 garlic clove, crushed
7.5 ml/1½ tsp Chinese five-spice
   powder
2.5 ml/½ tsp ground cinnamon
4 spring onions, sliced
sliced red chilli, to garnish (optional)

egg
noodles
celery stick
carrots
fennel
bulb
courgettes
red chilli
fresh root
ginger
five-spice
powder
cinnamon
garlic
spring onions

1 Bring a large pan of salted water to the boil. Add the noodles and cook for 2–3 minutes until just tender. Drain the noodles, return them to the pan and toss in a little of the oil. Set aside.

2 Cut the carrot and celery into julienne strips. Cut the fennel bulb in half and cut away the hard core. Cut into slices, then cut the slices into thin strips.

3 Heat the remaining oil in a wok until very hot. Add all the vegetables, including the chopped chilli, and stir-fry for 7–8 minutes. Add the ginger and garlic and stir-fry for 2 minutes, then add the spices. Cook for 1 minute.

4 Add the spring onions, stir-fry for 1 minute and then stir in 60 ml/4 tbsp warm water and cook for 1 minute. Stir in the noodles and toss well together. Serve sprinkled with sliced red chilli, if liked.

Noodles with Asparagus and Saffron Sauce

The asparagus, wine and cream give a distinctly French flavour to this elegant and delicious noodle dish.

Serves 4

INGREDIENTS
450 g/1 lb young asparagus
25 g/1 oz/2 tbsp butter
2 shallots, finely chopped
30 ml/2 tbsp white wine
250 ml/8 fl oz/1 cup double cream
pinch of saffron threads
grated rind and juice of ½ lemon
115 g/4 oz/1 cup garden peas
350 g/12 oz somen noodles
½ bunch chervil, roughly chopped
salt and freshly ground black pepper
grated Parmesan cheese (optional)

asparagus

saffron

shallots

butter

double cream

white wine

lemon

peas

somen noodles

1 Cut off the asparagus tips (about 5 cm/2 in length), then slice the remaining spears into short rounds. Soak the saffron in 30 ml/2 tbsp boiling water for a few minutes until softened.

Melt the butter in a saucepan, add the shallots and cook over a low heat for 3 minutes, until soft. Add the white wine, cream and saffron infusion. Bring to the boil, reduce the heat and simmer gently for 5 minutes or until the sauce thickens to a coating consistency. Add the lemon rind and juice, with salt and pepper to taste.

2 Bring a large saucepan of lightly salted water to the boil. Blanch the asparagus tips, scoop them out and add them to the sauce, then cook the peas and short asparagus rounds in the boiling water until just tender. Scoop them out and add to the sauce.

3 Cook the somen noodles in the same water until just tender, following the directions on the packet. Drain, place in a wide pan and pour the sauce over the top.

4 Toss the noodles with the sauce and vegetables, adding the chervil and more salt and pepper if needed. Finally, sprinkle with the grated Parmesan, if using, and serve hot.

COOK'S TIP

Frozen peas can easily be used instead of fresh peas. Add to the asparagus after 3–4 minutes and cook until tender.

Fried Noodles with Beansprouts and Baby Asparagus

This dish is simplicity itself with a wonderful contrast of textures and flavours. Use young asparagus which is beautifully tender and cooks in minutes.

Serves 2

INGREDIENTS

115 g/4 oz dried thin or medium
    egg noodles
60 ml/4 tbsp oil
1 small onion, chopped
2.5 cm/1 in fresh root ginger, grated
2 garlic cloves, crushed
175 g/6 oz young asparagus,
    trimmed
115 g/4 oz/½ cup beansprouts
4 spring onions, sliced
45 ml/3 tbsp light soy sauce
salt and freshly ground black pepper

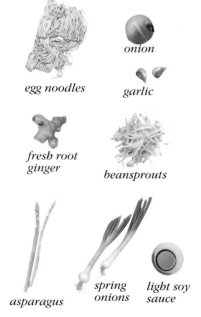

egg noodles

onion

garlic

fresh root ginger

beansprouts

asparagus

spring onions

light soy sauce

1 Bring a pan of salted water to the boil. Add the noodles and cook for 2–3 minutes, until just tender. Drain and toss in 30 ml/2 tbsp of the oil.

2 Heat the remaining oil in a wok or frying pan until very hot. Add the onion, ginger and garlic and stir-fry for 2–3 minutes. Add the asparagus and stir-fry for a further 2–3 minutes.

3 Add the noodles and beansprouts and stir-fry for 2 minutes.

4 Stir in the spring onions and soy sauce. Season to taste, adding salt sparingly as the soy sauce will add quite a salty flavour. Stir-fry for 1 minute, then serve at once.

Vegetable Chow Mein with Cashew Nuts

Chow mein is a popular dish that can be served with almost any type of Chinese vegetarian, meat or fish dish.

Serves 3–4

INGREDIENTS
30 ml/2 tbsp oil
50 g/2 oz/½ cup cashew nuts
2 carrots, cut into thin strips
3 celery sticks, cut into thin strips
1 green pepper, seeded and cut into thin strips
225 g/8 oz/1 cup beansprouts
225 g/8 oz dried medium or thin egg noodles
30 ml/2 tbsp toasted sesame seeds, to garnish

FOR THE LEMON SAUCE
30 ml/2 tbsp light soy sauce
15 ml/1 tbsp dry sherry
150 ml/¼ pint/⅔ cup vegetable stock
2 lemons
15 ml/1 tbsp sugar
10 ml/2 tsp cornflour

cashew nuts

carrots

green pepper

beansprouts

dried egg noodles

toasted sesame seeds

light soy sauce

lemon

1 Stir all the ingredients for the lemon sauce together in a jug. Bring a large saucepan of salted water to the boil.

2 Heat the oil in a wok or large heavy-based frying pan. Add the cashew nuts, toss quickly over a high heat until golden, then remove with a slotted spoon.

3 Add the carrots and celery to the pan and stir-fry for 4–5 minutes. Add the pepper and beansprouts and stir-fry for 2–3 minutes more. At the same time, cook the noodles in the pan of boiling water for 3 minutes, or according to the instructions on the packet. Drain well and place in a warmed serving dish.

4 Remove the vegetables from the pan with a slotted spoon. Pour in the sauce and cook for 2 minutes, stirring until thick. Return the vegetables to the pan, add the cashew nuts and stir quickly to coat in the sauce.

5 Spoon the vegetables and sauce over the noodles. Scatter with sesame seeds and serve.

Rice Noodles with Beef and Black Bean Sauce

This is an excellent combination – tender beef with a chilli black bean sauce tossed with silky-smooth rice noodles.

Serves 4

INGREDIENTS

450 g/1 lb fresh rice noodles
60 ml/4 tbsp oil
1 onion, finely sliced
2 garlic cloves, finely chopped
2 slices fresh root ginger, finely chopped
225 g/8 oz mixed peppers, seeded and sliced
350 g/12 oz rump steak, finely sliced against the grain
45 ml/3 tbsp fermented black beans, rinsed in warm water, drained and chopped
30 ml/2 tbsp dark soy sauce
30 ml/2 tbsp oyster sauce
15 ml/1 tbsp chilli black bean sauce
15 ml/1 tbsp cornflour
120 ml/4 fl oz/½ cup beef stock or water
2 spring onions, finely chopped, and 2 red chillies, seeded and finely sliced, to garnish

rice noodles • onion • fresh root ginger • garlic • red, yellow, green peppers • fermented black beans • dark soy sauce • oyster sauce • rump steak • red chillies • beef stock • spring onions

1 Rinse the noodles under hot water and drain well. Heat half the oil in a wok or frying pan, swirling it around. Add the onion, garlic, ginger and pepper slices.

2 Stir-fry for 3–5 minutes until the noodles are heated through, then remove and keep warm. Add the remaining oil to the wok and swirl to coat the pan. When hot, add the sliced beef and fermented black beans and stir-fry over a high heat for 5 minutes or until they are cooked.

3 In a small bowl, blend the soy sauce, oyster sauce and chilli black bean sauce with the cornflour and stock or water and stir until smooth. Add the mixture to the wok, together with the onion and peppers and cook, stirring, for 1 minute.

4 Add the noodles and mix lightly. Stir over a medium heat until the noodles are heated through. Adjust the seasoning if necessary. Serve at once, garnished with the chopped spring onions and finely sliced chillies.

Pork Chow Mein

Chow mein is a Cantonese speciality in which noodles are fried either by themselves or, as here, with meat and vegetables.

Serves 2–3

INGREDIENTS

175 g/6 oz medium egg noodles
350 g/12 oz pork fillet
30 ml/2 tbsp sunflower oil
15 ml/1 tbsp sesame oil
2 garlic cloves, crushed
8 spring onions, sliced
1 red pepper, seeded and roughly chopped
1 green pepper, seeded and roughly chopped
30 ml/2 tbsp dark soy sauce
45 ml/3 tbsp dry sherry
175 g/6 oz/¾ cup beansprouts
45 ml/3 tbsp chopped fresh flat-leaf parsley
15 ml/1 tbsp toasted sesame seeds

1 Soak the noodles according to the packet instructions. Drain well.

pork fillet

egg noodles

garlic

sesame oil

spring onions

red pepper

green pepper

dark soy sauce

dry sherry

beansprouts

flat-leaf parsley

toasted sesame seeds

2 Thinly slice the pork fillet. Heat the sunflower oil in a wok or large frying pan and cook the pork over a high heat until golden brown and cooked through.

3 Add the sesame oil to the pan, with the garlic, spring onions and peppers. Cook over a high heat for 3–4 minutes, or until the vegetables begin to soften.

4 Reduce the heat slightly and stir in the noodles, with the soy sauce and sherry. Stir-fry for 2 minutes. Add the beansprouts and cook for a further 1–2 minutes. Stir in the parsley and serve sprinkled with the sesame seeds.

Singapore Noodles

A delicious supper dish with a stunning mix of flavours and textures.

Serves 3–4

INGREDIENTS

225 g/8 oz dried egg noodles
45 ml/3 tbsp groundnut oil
1 onion, chopped
2.5 cm/1 in fresh root ginger,
   finely chopped
1 garlic clove, finely chopped
15 ml/1 tbsp Madras curry powder
2.5 ml/½ tsp salt
115 g/4 oz cooked chicken or pork,
   finely shredded
115 g/4 oz cooked peeled prawns
115 g/4 oz Chinese cabbage leaves,
   shredded
115 g/4 oz/½ cup beansprouts
60 ml/4 tbsp chicken stock
15–30 ml/1–2 tbsp dark soy sauce
1–2 red chillies, seeded and finely
   shredded
4 spring onions, thinly sliced

dried egg noodles   *onion*   *fresh root ginger*

garlic   *curry powder*   *chicken*

prawns   *Chinese cabbage*   *beansprouts*

chicken stock   *dark soy sauce*   *red chillies*

spring onions

1 Cook the noodles according to the packet instructions. Rinse thoroughly under cold water and drain well. Toss in 15 ml/1 tbsp of the oil and set aside.

2 Heat a wok until hot, add the remaining oil and swirl it around. Add the onion, ginger and garlic and stir-fry for about 2 minutes.

COOK'S TIP

If possible use groundnut oil for this dish or, alternatively, toss the noodles in sesame oil.

3 Add the curry powder and salt, stir-fry for 30 seconds, then add the egg noodles, chicken or pork and prawns. Stir-fry for 3–4 minutes.

4 Add the Chinese cabbage and beansprouts and stir-fry for 1–2 minutes. Stir in the stock and soy sauce to taste and toss well until evenly mixed. Serve at once, sprinkled with the shredded red chillies and spring onions.

Thai Fried Noodles

A staple of day-to-day Thai life, this dish is often served from the many food stalls that line any Thai street.

Serves 4

INGREDIENTS

175 g/6 oz ribbon rice noodles
30 ml/2 tbsp oil
2 garlic cloves, crushed
115 g/4 oz pork fillet, finely
    chopped
2 canned anchovy fillets, chopped
30 ml/2 tbsp lemon juice
45 ml/3 tbsp fish sauce
15 ml/1 tbsp caster sugar
225 g/8 oz beancurd, cubed
2 eggs, beaten
75 g/3 oz cooked peeled prawns
115 g/4 oz/½ cup beansprouts
75 g/3 oz/½ cup unsalted roasted
    peanuts
75 ml/5 tbsp chopped fresh
    coriander
fresh coriander sprigs, to garnish
    (optional)
dried flaked chillies and fish sauce,
    to serve

ribbon rice
noodles

garlic

pork fillet

lemon
juice

fish sauce

anchovy
fillets

beancurd

eggs

caster sugar

prawns

beansprouts

peanuts

fresh
coriander

dried flaked
chillies

1 Soak the noodles in boiling water, according to the packet instructions; drain well.

2 Heat the oil in a wok or large frying pan and cook the garlic until golden. Add the pork and stir-fry until cooked through and golden.

3 Reduce the heat slightly and stir in the anchovies, lemon juice, fish sauce and sugar. Bring to a gentle simmer.

4 Stir in the beancurd, taking care not to break it up. Fold in the noodles gently, until they are coated in the liquid.

5 Make a gap at the side of the pan and add the beaten eggs. Allow them to scramble slightly and then stir them into the noodles.

6 Stir in the prawns and most of the beansprouts, peanuts and coriander. Cook until piping hot. Serve the noodles topped with the remaining beansprouts, peanuts and chopped coriander, sprinkled with a few dried flaked chillies and more fish sauce, to taste. Garnish with fresh coriander sprigs, if liked.

Five-flavour Noodles

The Japanese title for this dish is *gomoku yakisoba*, meaning five different ingredients: noodles, pork, cabbage, beansprouts and peppers.

Serves 4

INGREDIENTS

300 g/11 oz dried Chinese thin egg
   noodles or 500 g/1¼ lb fresh
   yakisoba noodles
200 g/7 oz pork fillet, thinly sliced
25 ml/1½ tbsp oil
10 g/¼ oz fresh root ginger, grated
1 garlic clove, crushed
200 g/7 oz/1¾ cups green cabbage,
   roughly chopped
115 g/4 oz/½ cup beansprouts
1 green pepper, seeded and cut into
   fine strips
1 red pepper, seeded and cut into
   fine strips
salt and freshly ground black pepper
20 ml/4 tsp ao-nori seaweed, to
   garnish (optional)

FOR THE SEASONING

60 ml/4 tbsp Worcestershire sauce
15 ml/1 tbsp light soy sauce
15 ml/1 tbsp oyster sauce
15 ml/1 tbsp sugar
white pepper

thin egg noodles

fresh root ginger

garlic

pork fillet

beansprouts

green and red peppers

light soy sauce

1 Boil the egg noodles according to the packet instructions and drain. Using a sharp chopping knife, carefully cut the pork fillet into 3–4-cm/1¼–1½-in strips and season with plenty of salt and pepper. Next, heat 7.5 ml/1½ tsp of the oil in a large frying pan or wok and stir-fry the pork until just cooked, then transfer to a dish.

2 Wipe the pan with kitchen paper, and heat the remaining oil. Add the ginger, garlic and cabbage and stir-fry for 1 minute.

3 Add the beansprouts and stir until softened, then add the green and red peppers and stir-fry for 1 minute.

4 Return the pork to the pan and add the noodles. Stir in all the seasoning ingredients together with a little white pepper. Stir-fry for 2–3 minutes. Sprinkle with the ao-nori seaweed, if using.

Indonesian Courgettes with Noodles

Any courgette or member of the squash family can be used in this quick and refreshing Indonesian dish, called *oseng oseng*.

Serves 4–6

INGREDIENTS
450 g/1 lb courgettes, sliced
1 onion, finely sliced
1 garlic clove, finely chopped
30 ml/2 tbsp sunflower oil
2.5 ml/½ tsp ground turmeric
2 tomatoes, chopped
45 ml/3 tbsp water
115 g/4 oz cooked, peeled prawns, (optional)
25 g/1 oz cellophane noodles
salt

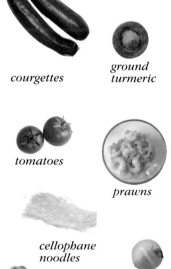

courgettes

ground turmeric

tomatoes

prawns

cellophane noodles

onion

garlic

1 Use a potato peeler to cut thin strips from the outside of each courgette. Cut them in neat slices. Set the courgettes on one side.

2 Fry the onion and garlic in hot oil; do not allow them to brown. Add the turmeric, courgette slices, chopped tomatoes, water and prawns, if using.

3 Put the noodles in a pan and pour over boiling water to cover, leave for a minute and then drain. Cut the noodles in 5 cm/2 in lengths and add to the vegetables.

4 Cover with a lid and allow the noodles to cook in their own steam for 2–3 minutes. Gently toss everything well together. Season with salt to taste and serve while still hot.

COOK'S TIP
Courgettes should be firm with a glossy, healthy looking skin. Avoid any that feel squashy or generally look limp, as they will be dry and not worth using.

Gingered Chicken Noodles

A blend of ginger, spices and coconut milk flavours, this delicious supper dish is made in minutes. For a real oriental touch, add a little fish sauce to taste, just before serving.

Serves 2–4

INGREDIENTS

350 g/12 oz boneless, skinless
   chicken breasts
225 g/8 oz courgettes
275 g/10 oz aubergine
about 30 ml/2 tbsp oil
5 cm/2 in fresh root ginger,
   finely chopped
6 spring onions, sliced
10 ml/2 tsp Thai green curry paste
400 ml/14 fl oz/1⅔ cups coconut
   milk
475 ml/16 fl oz/2 cups chicken stock
115 g/4 oz medium egg noodles
45 ml/3 tbsp chopped fresh
   coriander
15 ml/1 tbsp lemon juice
salt and white pepper
chopped fresh coriander, to garnish

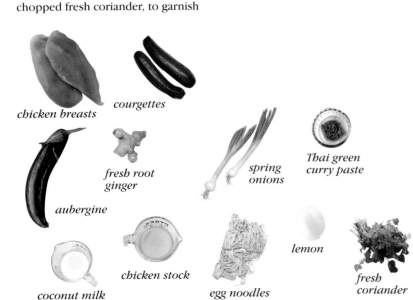

chicken breasts   *courgettes*

aubergine

fresh root ginger

spring onions

Thai green curry paste

coconut milk

chicken stock

egg noodles

lemon

fresh coriander

1 Cut the chicken into bite-size pieces. Halve the courgettes lengthways and roughly chop them. Cut the aubergine into similarly sized pieces.

2 Heat the oil in a large saucepan or wok and cook the chicken pieces, in batches if necessary, until golden. Remove the pieces with a slotted spoon and leave to drain on kitchen paper.

COOK'S TIP

Very popular throughout South-east Asia, fish sauce can range in colour from ochre to deep brown. It is a pungent liquid that has a strong and salty flavour, so should only be used sparingly if unsure.

3 Add a little more oil, if necessary, and cook the ginger and spring onions for 3 minutes. Add the courgettes and cook for 2–3 minutes. Stir in the curry paste and cook for 1 minute. Add the coconut milk, stock, aubergine and chicken, and simmer for 10 minutes.

4 Add the noodles and cook for a further 5 minutes, or until the chicken is cooked and the noodles are tender. Stir in the chopped coriander and lemon juice and adjust the seasoning. Serve garnished with chopped coriander.

Bamie Goreng

This fried noodle dish from Indonesia is wonderfully accommodating. To the basic recipe you can add other vegetables, such as mushrooms, tiny pieces of courgette, broccoli, leeks or beansprouts, if you prefer.

Serves 6

INGREDIENTS
450 g/1 lb dried egg noodles
1 boneless, skinless chicken breast
115 g/4 oz pork fillet
115 g/4 oz calves' liver (optional)
2 eggs, beaten
90 ml/6 tbsp oil
25 g/1 oz/2 tbsp butter
2 garlic cloves, crushed
115 g/4 oz cooked, peeled prawns
115 g/4 oz spinach or Chinese leaves
2 celery sticks, finely sliced
4 spring onions, cut into strips
about 60 ml/4 tbsp chicken stock
dark and light soy sauce
1 onion, thinly sliced
oil, for deep-frying
salt and freshly ground black pepper
celery leaves, to garnish

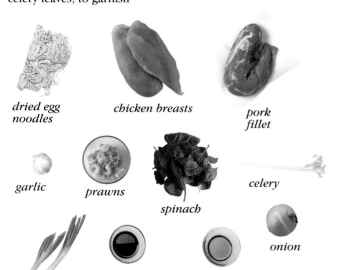

dried egg noodles *chicken breasts* *pork fillet*

garlic *prawns* *celery*

spinach

spring onions *dark soy sauce* *light soy sauce* *onion*

1 Cook the noodles in boiling, salted water for 3–4 minutes. Drain, rinse with cold water and drain again. Set aside until required.

2 Using a small, sharp chopping knife, finely slice the chicken breast, pork fillet and calves' liver, if using.

3 Season the eggs. Heat 5 ml/1 tsp of the oil with the butter in a small pan until melted and then stir in the eggs and keep stirring until scrambled. Set aside.

4 Heat the remaining oil in a wok and fry the garlic with the chicken, pork and liver for 2–3 minutes. Add the prawns, spinach or Chinese leaves, celery and spring onions, tossing well. Add the noodles and toss well. Add enough stock to moisten the noodles and dark and light soy sauce to taste.

5 In a separate wok or deep-fat fryer, deep-fry the onion until crisp and golden, turning constantly. Drain well. Stir the scrambled egg into the noodles and serve garnished with the deep-fried onion and celery leaves.

Beef Noodles with Orange and Ginger

Stir-frying is one of the best ways to cook with the minimum of fat. It's also one of the quickest ways to cook, but you do need to choose tender meat.

Serves 4

INGREDIENTS
450 g/1 lb lean beef, e.g. rump,
   fillet or sirloin steak, cut into
   thin strips
finely grated rind and juice of
   1 orange
15 ml/1 tbsp light soy sauce
5 ml/1 tsp cornflour
2.5 cm/1 in fresh root ginger,
   finely chopped
175 g/6 oz rice noodles
10 ml/2 tsp sesame oil
15 ml/1 tbsp sunflower oil
1 large carrot, cut into thin strips
2 spring onions, thinly sliced

rump steak

orange

light soy sauce

fresh root ginger

carrot

sesame oil

spring onions

rice noodles

1 Place the beef in a bowl and sprinkle over the orange rind and juice. If possible, leave to marinate for at least 30 minutes.

2 Drain the liquid from the meat and set aside, then mix the meat with the soy sauce, cornflour and ginger. Cook the noodles according to the instructions on the packet. Drain well, toss with the sesame oil and keep warm.

3 Heat the sunflower oil in a wok or large frying pan and add the beef. Stir-fry for 1 minute until lightly coloured, then add the carrot and stir-fry for a further 2–3 minutes.

4 Stir in the spring onions and the reserved liquid from the meat, then cook, stirring, until boiling and thickened. Serve hot with the rice noodles.

Stir-fried Sweet-and-Sour Chicken

As well as quick, this South East Asian dish is decidedly tasty and you will find yourself making it again and again.

Serves 3–4

INGREDIENTS

275 g/10 oz dried medium egg
   noodles
30 ml/2 tbsp oil
3 spring onions, chopped
1 garlic clove, crushed
2.5 cm/1 in fresh root ginger, grated
5 ml/1 tsp paprika
5 ml/1 tsp ground coriander
3 boneless chicken breasts, sliced
225 g/8 oz sugar snap peas, topped
   and tailed
115 g/4 oz baby sweetcorn, halved
225 g/8 oz/1 cup beansprouts
15 ml/1 tbsp cornflour
45 ml/3 tbsp light soy sauce
45 ml/3 tbsp lemon juice
15 ml/1 tbsp sugar
45 ml/3 tbsp chopped fresh
   coriander, to garnish

egg noodles

spring onions

garlic

ground coriander

beansprouts

chicken breasts

fresh coriander

1 Bring a large saucepan of salted water to the boil. Add the noodles and cook according to the packet instructions. Drain thoroughly, cover and keep warm.

2 Heat the oil. Add the spring onions and cook over a gentle heat. Mix in the next five ingredients, then stir-fry for 3–4 minutes. Add the next three ingredients and cook briefly. Add the noodles.

3 Combine the cornflour, soy sauce, lemon juice and sugar in a small bowl. Add to the wok and simmer briefly to thicken. Serve garnished with chopped fresh coriander.

COOK'S TIP
Large wok lids are cumbersome and can be difficult to store in a small kitchen. Consider placing a circle of greaseproof paper against the food surface to keep cooking juices in.

Cellophane Noodles with Pork

Cellophane noodles absorb liquid at four times their weight and have the ability of taking on the flavour of the ingredients they are cooked with.

Serves 3–4

INGREDIENTS

115 g/4 oz cellophane noodles
4 dried Chinese black mushrooms
225 g/8 oz pork fillet
30 ml/2 tbsp dark soy sauce
30 ml/2 tbsp Chinese rice wine
2 garlic cloves, crushed
15 ml/1 tbsp grated fresh root
    ginger
5 ml/1 tsp chilli oil
45 ml/3 tbsp oil
4–6 spring onions, chopped
5 ml/1 tsp cornflour blended with
    175 ml/6 fl oz/¾ cup chicken
    stock or water
30 ml/2 tbsp chopped fresh
    coriander
salt and freshly ground black pepper
coriander sprigs, to garnish

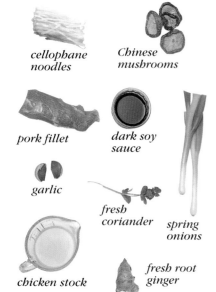

cellophane noodles

Chinese mushrooms

pork fillet

dark soy sauce

garlic

fresh coriander

spring onions

chicken stock

fresh root ginger

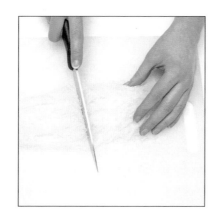

1 Put the noodles and mushrooms in separate bowls and cover them with warm water. Leave to soak for 15–20 minutes, until soft; drain well. Cut the noodles into 13-cm/5-in lengths. Squeeze any water from the mushrooms, discard the stems and finely chop the caps.

2 Cut the pork into very small cubes. Put into a bowl with the soy sauce, rice wine, garlic, ginger and chilli oil, then leave for about 15 minutes. Drain, reserving the marinade.

3 Heat the oil in a wok and add the pork and mushrooms. Stir-fry for 3 minutes. Add the spring onions and stir-fry for 1 minute. Stir in the chicken stock, marinade and seasoning.

4 Add the noodles and stir-fry for about 2 minutes, until the noodles absorb most of the liquid and the pork is cooked through. Stir in the coriander. Serve garnished with coriander sprigs.

Noodles with Ginger and Coriander

Here is a simple noodle dish that goes well with most oriental dishes. It can also be served as a snack for 2–3 people.

Serves 4

INGREDIENTS
handful of fresh coriander
225 g/8 oz dried egg noodles
45 ml/3 tbsp oil
5 cm/2 in fresh root ginger, cut into
    fine shreds
6–8 spring onions, cut into shreds
30 ml/2 tbsp light soy sauce
salt and freshly ground black pepper

fresh coriander

dried egg noodles

fresh root ginger

spring onions

light soy sauce

1 Strip the leaves from the coriander stalks. Pile them on to a chopping board and coarsely chop them using a cleaver or large, sharp knife.

2 Cook the noodles according to the packet instructions. Rinse under cold water, drain well and then toss in 15 ml/1 tbsp of the oil.

3 Heat a wok until hot, add the remaining oil and swirl it around. Add the ginger and stir-fry for a few seconds, then add the noodles and spring onions. Stir-fry for 3–4 minutes, until hot.

4 Sprinkle over the soy sauce, coriander and seasoning. Toss well and serve at once.

COOK'S TIP

As with many Thai, Singapore or Malaysian dishes, for best results use groundnut oil. Alternatively fry vegetables in sunflower oil, but toss noodles in sesame oil.

Lemon Grass Prawns on Crisp Noodle Cake

For an elegant meal, make four individual noodle cakes instead of one.

Serves 4

INGREDIENTS

300 g/11 oz thin egg noodles
60 ml/4 tbsp oil
500 g/1¼ lb medium raw king
  prawns, peeled and deveined
2.5 ml/½ tsp ground coriander
15 ml/1 tbsp ground turmeric
2 garlic cloves, finely chopped
2 slices fresh root ginger, finely
  chopped
2 lemon grass stalks, finely chopped
2 shallots, finely chopped
15 ml/1 tbsp tomato purée
250 ml/8 fl oz/1 cup coconut cream
15–30 ml/1–2 tbsp fresh lime juice
15–30 ml/1–2 tbsp fish sauce
4–6 kaffir lime leaves (optional)
1 cucumber, peeled, seeded and cut
  into 5-cm/2-in sticks
1 tomato, seeded and cut into strips
2 red chillies, seeded and finely
  sliced
salt and freshly ground black pepper
2 spring onions, cut into thin strips,
  and a few coriander sprigs, to
  garnish

1 Cook the egg noodles in a saucepan of boiling water until just tender. Drain, rinse under cold running water and drain well.

2 Heat 15 ml/1 tbsp of the oil in a large frying pan. Add the noodles, distributing them evenly, and fry for 4–5 minutes, until crisp and golden. Turn the noodle cake over and fry the other side. Alternatively, make four individual cakes. Keep warm.

3 In a bowl, toss the prawns with the ground coriander, turmeric, garlic, ginger and lemon grass. Season to taste. Heat the remaining oil in a frying pan. Add the shallots, fry for 1 minute, then add the prawns and fry for 2 minutes more before removing with a slotted spoon.

egg noodles
raw king prawns
ground coriander
ground turmeric
garlic
fresh root ginger
lemon grass
shallots
tomato purée
coconut cream
kaffir lime leaves
fish sauce
cucumber
tomato
lime
red chillies
spring onions
fresh coriander

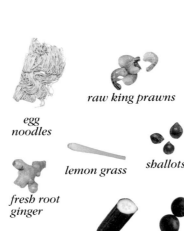

4 Stir the tomato purée and coconut cream into the juices in the pan. Stir in lime juice to taste and season with the fish sauce. Bring the sauce to a simmer, return the prawns, then add the kaffir lime leaves, if using, and the cucumber. Simmer until the prawns are cooked.

5 Add the tomato, stir until just warmed through, then add the chillies. Serve on top of the crisp noodle cake(s), garnished with strips of spring onions and coriander sprigs.

Japanese Sweet Soy Salmon with Noodles

Teriyaki sauce forms the marinade for the salmon in this recipe. Served with soft-fried noodles, it makes a stunning dish.

Serves 3–4

INGREDIENTS
350 g/12 oz salmon fillet
30 ml/2 tbsp Japanese soy sauce (shoyu)
30 ml/2 tbsp sake
60 ml/4 tbsp mirin or sweet sherry
5 ml/1 tsp light brown soft sugar
10 ml/2 tsp grated fresh root ginger
3 garlic cloves, 1 crushed and 2 sliced into rounds
30 ml/2 tbsp groundnut oil
225 g/8 oz dried egg noodles, cooked and drained
50 g/2 oz alfalfa sprouts
30 ml/2 tbsp sesame seeds, lightly toasted

salmon

Japanese soy sauce

sake

garlic

mirin

fresh root ginger

noodles

groundnut oil

alfalfa sprouts

sesame seeds

COOK'S TIP

It is important to scrape the marinade off the fish as any remaining pieces of ginger or garlic would burn during grilling and spoil the finished dish.

1 Using a sharp chopping knife, cut the salmon into thin slices, then place in a shallow dish.

2 In a bowl, mix together the soy sauce, sake, mirin or sherry, sugar, ginger and crushed garlic. Pour over the salmon, cover and leave for 30 minutes.

3 Preheat the grill. Drain the salmon, scraping off and reserving the marinade. Place the salmon in a single layer on a baking sheet. Cook under the grill for 2–3 minutes without turning.

4 Meanwhile, heat a wok until hot, add the oil and swirl it around. Add the garlic rounds and cook until golden brown but not burnt.

5 Add the cooked noodles and reserved marinade to the wok and stir-fry for 3–4 minutes, until the marinade has reduced slightly to a syrupy glaze and coats the noodles.

6 Toss in the alfalfa sprouts, then remove immediately from the heat. Transfer to warmed serving plates and top with the salmon. Sprinkle with the toasted sesame seeds. Serve at once.

Celebration Thai Noodles

This Thai speciality, called *mee krob*, is a crisp tangle of fried rice vermicelli tossed in a piquant sauce. It is served at weddings and other special occasions.

Serves 4

INGREDIENTS

oil, for deep-frying
175 g/6 oz rice vermicelli
15 ml/1 tbsp chopped garlic
4–6 dried chillies, seeded and chopped
30 ml/2 tbsp chopped shallot
15 ml/1 tbsp dried shrimps, rinsed
115 g/4 oz minced pork
115 g/4 oz uncooked, peeled prawns, chopped
30 ml/2 tbsp brown bean sauce
30 ml/2 tbsp rice wine vinegar
45 ml/3 tbsp fish sauce
75 g/3 tbsp palm sugar or soft brown sugar
30 ml/2 tbsp tamarind or lime juice
115 g/4 oz/½ cup beansprouts

FOR THE GARNISH

2 spring onions, cut into thin strips
fresh coriander leaves
2 heads pickled garlic (optional)
2-egg omelette, rolled and sliced
2 red chillies, seeded and chopped

rice vermicelli noodles
garlic
chillies
dried shrimps
minced pork
uncooked prawns
beansprouts
spring onions

1 Heat the oil in a wok. Break the rice vermicelli apart into small handfuls about 7.5 cm/3 in long. Deep-fry in the hot oil until they puff up. Remove and drain on kitchen paper.

2 Leave 30 ml/2 tbsp of the hot oil in the wok, add the garlic, chillies, shallots and dried shrimps. Fry until fragrant, then add the minced pork and stir-fry for about 3–4 minutes, until it is no longer pink. Add the prawns and fry for a further 2 minutes. Transfer the mixture to a plate and set aside.

3 Stir the brown bean sauce, vinegar, fish sauce and palm or brown sugar into the wok. Bring to a gentle boil, stir to dissolve the sugar and cook until thick and syrupy. Add the tamarind or lime juice and adjust the seasoning. It should be sweet, sour and salty.

4 Reduce the heat. Add the pork and prawn mixture and the beansprouts to the sauce, stir to mix and then add the rice noodles, tossing gently to coat them with the sauce. Transfer the noodles to a platter. Garnish with spring onions, fresh coriander leaves, omelette strips, red chillies and pickled garlic, if liked.

King Prawn Thai Noodles

This delicately flavoured dish is considered one of the national dishes of Thailand, where it is known as *phat thai*.

Serves 4–6

INGREDIENTS

350 g/12 oz rice noodles
45 ml/3 tbsp oil
15 ml/1 tbsp chopped garlic
16 uncooked king prawns, peeled, tails left intact and deveined
2 eggs, lightly beaten
15 ml/1 tbsp dried shrimps, rinsed
30 ml/2 tbsp pickled mooli (white radish)
50 g/2 oz fried beancurd, cut into small slivers
2.5 ml/½ tsp dried chilli flakes
115 g/4 oz Chinese chives, cut into 5-cm/2-in lengths
225 g/8 oz/1 cup beansprouts
50 g/2 oz roasted peanuts, coarsely ground
5 ml/1 tsp sugar
15 ml/1 tbsp dark soy sauce
30 ml/2 tbsp fish sauce
30 ml/2 tbsp tamarind or lime juice
fresh coriander leaves, to garnish
lime wedges, to serve (optional)

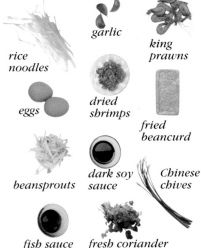

rice noodles

garlic

king prawns

eggs

dried shrimps

fried beancurd

beansprouts

dark soy sauce

Chinese chives

fish sauce

fresh coriander

1 Soak the noodles in warm water for 20–30 minutes, then drain. Heat 15 ml/1 tbsp of the oil in a wok or large frying pan. Add the garlic and fry until golden. Stir in the prawns and cook for about 1–2 minutes, until pink, tossing from time to time. Transfer to a plate.

2 Heat a further 15 ml/1 tbsp of oil in the wok. Add the eggs, tilting the wok to spread them into a thin sheet. Scramble and then transfer to a plate and set aside. Heat the remaining oil and add the dried shrimps, pickled mooli, beancurd and dried chilli flakes. Stir briefly.

3 Add the noodles and stir-fry for 5 minutes, then add the Chinese chives, half the beansprouts and half the peanuts. Season with the sugar, soy sauce, fish sauce and tamarind or lime juice. Mix well.

4 When the noodles are cooked through, return the prawns and cooked eggs to the wok and mix together. Serve garnished with the rest of the bean-sprouts, peanuts and the coriander leaves, with lime wedges if you wish.

Beef and Vegetables in Table-top Broth

The perfect introduction to Japanese cooking, this dish is well suited to party gatherings.

Serves 4–6

INGREDIENTS
450 g/1 lb sirloin beef, trimmed
1.75 litres/3 pints/7½ cups kombu and bonito stock or ½ sachet instant dashi powder, or ½ vegetable stock cube with 1.75 litres/3 pints/7½ cups water
150 g/5 oz carrots
6 spring onions, trimmed and sliced
150 g/5 oz Chinese leaves, roughly shredded
225 g/8 oz mooli (white radish), peeled and shredded
275 g/10 oz udon or fine wheat noodles, cooked
115 g/4 oz canned bamboo shoots, sliced
175 g/6 oz beancurd, cut into large dice
10 shiitake mushrooms

FOR THE SESAME DIPPING SAUCE
50 g/2 oz sesame seeds or 30 ml/2 tbsp tahini paste
120 ml/4 fl oz/½ cup instant dashi stock or vegetable stock
60 ml/4 tbsp dark soy sauce
10 ml/2 tsp sugar
30 ml/2 tbsp sake (optional)
10 ml/2 tsp wasabi powder (optional)

FOR THE PONZU DIPPING SAUCE
75 ml/5 tbsp lemon juice
15 ml/1 tbsp rice wine or white wine vinegar
75 ml/5 tbsp dark soy sauce
15 ml/1 tbsp tamari sauce
15 ml/1 tbsp mirin or 1 tsp sugar
1.5 ml/¼ tsp instant dashi powder or ¼ vegetable stock cube

beef

kombu and bonito stock

carrots

spring onions

Chinese leaves

udon noodles

bamboo shoots

beancurd

shiitake mushrooms

sesame seeds

dark soy sauce

sake

lemon juice

mirin

1 Slice the meat thinly with a large knife or cleaver. Arrange neatly on a plate, cover and set aside. In a Japanese donabe, or any other covered, flameproof casserole that is unglazed on the outside, bring the kombu and bonito stock, dashi powder or stock cube and water to the boil. Cover and simmer for 8–10 minutes. Place at the table, standing on its own heat source.

2 To prepare the vegetables, bring a saucepan of salted water to the boil. Peel the carrots and with a canelle knife cut a series of grooves along their length. Slice the carrots thinly and blanch for 2–3 minutes. Blanch the spring onions, Chinese leaves and mooli for the same time. Arrange the vegetables with the noodles, bamboo shoots and beancurd. Slice the mushrooms.

3 To make the sesame dipping sauce, dry-fry the sesame seeds, if using, in a heavy frying pan, taking care not to burn them. Grind the seeds smoothly using a pestle and mortar with a rough surface. Alternatively, you can use tahini paste. Add the remaining sesame dipping sauce ingredients, combine well, then pour into a shallow dish.

4 To make the ponzu dipping sauce, put the ingredients into a screw-top jar and shake well. Provide your guests with chopsticks and individual bowls, so they can help themselves to what they want. The idea is to cook their choice of meat and vegetables in the stock and flavour these with either the sesame or ponzu dipping sauces. Towards the end of the meal, each guest takes a portion of noodles and ladles the well-flavoured stock over them.

Clay Pot of Chilli Squid and Noodles

This dish is delicious in its own right, or served as part of a larger Chinese meal, with other meat or fish dishes and rice.

Serves 2–4

INGREDIENTS
675 g/1½ lb fresh squid
30 ml/2 tbsp oil
3 slices fresh root ginger, finely chopped
2 garlic cloves, finely chopped
1 red onion, finely sliced
1 carrot, finely sliced
1 celery stick, sliced diagonally
50 g/2 oz sugar snap peas, topped and tailed
5 ml/1 tsp sugar
15 ml/1 tbsp chilli bean paste
2.5 ml/½ tsp chilli powder
75 g/3 oz cellophane noodles, soaked in hot water until soft
120 ml/4 fl oz/½ cup chicken stock or water
15 ml/1 tbsp light soy sauce
15 ml/1 tbsp oyster sauce
5 ml/1 tsp sesame oil
pinch of salt
fresh coriander leaves, to garnish

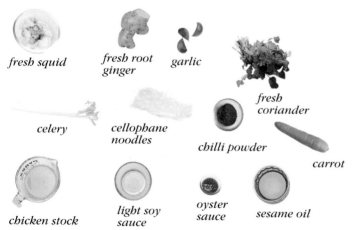

fresh squid *fresh root ginger* *garlic*

celery *cellophane noodles* *fresh coriander*

chilli powder

carrot

chicken stock *light soy sauce* *oyster sauce* *sesame oil*

1 Prepare the squid. Holding the body in one hand, gently pull away the head and tentacles. Discard the head; trim and reserve the tentacles. Remove the 'quill' from inside the body of the squid. Peel off the brown skin on the outside. Rub salt into the squid and wash under water. Cut the body of the squid into rings or split it open lengthways, score criss-cross patterns on the inside of the body and cut it into 5 x 4-cm/2 x 1½-in pieces.

2 Heat the oil in a large, flameproof casserole or wok. Add the ginger, garlic and onion and fry for 1–2 minutes. Add the squid, carrot, celery and sugar snap peas. Fry until the squid curls up. Season with salt and sugar and then stir in the chilli bean paste and powder. Transfer the mixture to a bowl and set aside until required. Drain the soaked noodles and add to the casserole or wok.

3 Stir in the chicken stock or water, light soy sauce and oyster sauce. Cover and cook over a medium heat for 10 minutes or until the noodles are tender. Return the squid and vegetable mixture to the pot.

4 Cover and cook for a further 5–6 minutes, until all the flavours are combined. Season to taste.

5 Spoon the mixture into a warmed clay pot and drizzle with the sesame oil. Sprinkle with the coriander leaves and serve immediately.

COOK'S TIP

These noodles have a smooth, light texture that readily absorbs the other flavours in the dish. To vary the flavour, the vegetables can be altered according to what is available.

Tiger Prawn and Lap Cheong Noodles

Lap cheong is a special air-dried Chinese sausage. It is available from most Chinese supermarkets. If you cannot buy it, replace with diced ham, chorizo or salami.

Serves 4–6

INGREDIENTS
45 ml/3 tbsp oil
2 garlic cloves, sliced
5 ml/1 tsp chopped fresh root
    ginger
2 red chillies, seeded and chopped
2 lap cheong, about 75 g/3 oz,
    rinsed and sliced (optional)
1 boneless chicken breast, thinly
    sliced
16 uncooked tiger prawns, peeled,
    tails left intact and deveined
115 g/4 oz green beans
225 g/8 oz/1 cup beansprouts
50 g/2 oz Chinese chives
450 g/1 lb egg noodles, cooked in
    boiling water until tender
30 ml/2 tbsp dark soy sauce
15 ml/1 tbsp oyster sauce
salt and freshly ground black pepper
15 ml/1 tbsp sesame oil
2 spring onions, cut into strips, and
    fresh coriander leaves, to garnish

red chillies

chicken breast

prawns

garlic

green beans

beansprouts

Chinese
chives

egg
noodles

dark soy
sauce

fresh root
ginger

oyster
sauce   sesame oil

spring onions

coriander

COOK'S TIP
Chinese chives, sometimes called garlic chives, have a delicate garlic/onion flavour. If they are not available, use the green parts of spring onions.

1 Heat 15 ml/1 tbsp of the oil in a wok or large frying pan and fry the garlic, ginger and chillies.

2 Add the lap cheong, chicken, prawns and beans. Stir-fry for about 2 minutes over a high heat or until the chicken and prawns are cooked. Transfer the mixture to a bowl and set aside.

3 Heat the remaining oil in the wok and add the beansprouts and Chinese chives. Stir-fry for 1–2 minutes.

4 Add the noodles and toss and stir to mix. Season with soy sauce, oyster sauce, salt and pepper.

5 Return the prawn mixture to the wok. Reheat and mix well with the noodles. Stir in the sesame oil. Serve garnished with spring onions and coriander leaves.

Luxury Fried Noodles

This makes a tasty side dish for three to four people or a meal for two people, served with just a separate vegetable or meat dish.

Serves 2–4

INGREDIENTS
40 g/1½ oz dried Chinese
    mushrooms
275 g/10 oz fine egg noodles
15 ml/1 tbsp sesame oil
45 ml/3 tbsp oil
2 garlic cloves, crushed
1 onion, chopped
2 green chillies, seeded and thinly
    sliced
15 ml/1 tbsp curry powder
175 g/6 oz green beans
115 g/4 oz Chinese leaves, thinly
    shredded
6 spring onions, sliced
45 ml/3 tbsp dark soy sauce
175 g/6 oz cooked, peeled prawns
salt

Chinese mushrooms

egg noodles

sesame oil *garlic* *onion*

green chillies *curry powder*

green beans *Chinese leaves*

prawns *dark soy sauce* *spring onions*

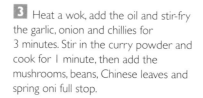

1 Place the mushrooms in a bowl. Cover with warm water and soak for 30 minutes. Drain, reserving 45 ml/3 tbsp of the soaking water, then slice, discarding the stems.

2 Cook the noodles in a pan of lightly salted boiling water according to the directions on the packet. Drain, place in a bowl and toss with the sesame oil.

3 Heat a wok, add the oil and stir-fry the garlic, onion and chillies for 3 minutes. Stir in the curry powder and cook for 1 minute, then add the mushrooms, beans, Chinese leaves and spring oni full stop.

4 Add the noodles, soy sauce, reserved mushroom soaking water and prawns. Toss over the heat for 2–3 minutes, until the noodles and prawns are heated through, then serve.

Chicken Curry with Rice Vermicelli

Lemon grass gives this South East Asian curry a wonderful, lemony flavour and fragrance.

Serves 4

INGREDIENTS

1 chicken, about 1.5 kg/3–3½ lb
225 g/8 oz sweet potatoes
60 ml/4 tbsp oil
1 onion, finely sliced
3 garlic cloves, crushed
30–45 ml/2–3 tbsp Thai curry
   powder
5 ml/1 tsp sugar
10 ml/2 tsp fish sauce
600 ml/1 pint/2½ cups coconut milk
1 lemon grass stalk, cut in half
350 g/12 oz rice vermicelli, soaked
   in hot water until soft
salt

FOR THE GARNISH

115 g/4 oz/½ cup beansprouts
2 spring onions, finely sliced
   diagonally
2 red chillies, seeded and finely
   sliced
8–10 mint leaves

Thai curry powder

chicken

coconut milk

rice vermicelli noodles

lemon grass

beansprouts

mint leaves

red chillies

spring onions

1 Skin the chicken. Cut the flesh into small pieces. Peel the sweet potatoes and cut them into large chunks, about the size of the chicken pieces.

2 Heat half the oil in a large, heavy saucepan. Add the onion and garlic and fry until the onion softens. Add the chicken pieces and stir-fry until they change colour. Stir in the curry powder. Season with salt and sugar and mix thoroughly, then add the fish sauce, coconut milk and lemon grass. Cook over a low heat for 15 minutes.

3 Meanwhile, heat the remaining oil in a large frying pan. Fry the sweet potatoes until lightly golden. Using a slotted spoon, add them to the chicken. Cook for 10–15 minutes more, or until both the chicken and sweet potatoes are tender.

4 Drain the rice vermicelli and cook them in a saucepan of boiling water for 3–5 minutes. Drain well. Place in shallow bowls, with the chicken curry. Garnish with beansprouts, spring onions, chillies and mint leaves, and serve.

Birthday Noodles with Hoisin Lamb

In China, the noodles served at birthday celebrations are left long: it is held that cutting them might shorten one's life.

Serves 4

INGREDIENTS
350 g/12 oz thick egg noodles
1 kg/2¼ lb lean neck fillets of lamb
30 ml/2 tbsp oil
115 g/4 oz fine green beans,
   blanched
salt and freshly ground black pepper
2 hard-boiled eggs, halved, and
   2 spring onions, finely shredded,
   to garnish

FOR THE MARINADE
2 garlic cloves, crushed
10 ml/2 tsp grated fresh root ginger
30 ml/2 tbsp dark soy sauce
30 ml/2 tbsp rice wine
1–2 dried red chillies
30 ml/2 tbsp oil

FOR THE SAUCE
15 ml/1 tbsp cornflour
30 ml/2 tbsp dark soy sauce
30 ml/2 tbsp rice wine
grated rind and juice of ½ orange
15 ml/1 tbsp hoisin sauce
15 ml/1 tbsp wine vinegar
5 ml/1 tsp soft, light brown sugar

orange *green beans* *lamb fillet* *spring onions* *garlic*

fresh root ginger *dark soy sauce* *hoisin sauce* *eggs* *wine vinegar* *thick egg noodles*

1 Bring a large saucepan of water to the boil. Add the noodles and cook for 2 minutes only. Drain, rinse under cold water and drain again. Set aside. Cut the lamb into 5-cm/2-in-thick medallions. Mix the ingredients for the marinade in a large, shallow dish. Add the lamb and leave to marinate for at least 4 hours or overnight.

2 Heat the oil in a heavy-based saucepan or flameproof casserole. Fry the lamb for 5 minutes, until browned. Add just enough water to cover the meat. Bring to the boil, skim, then reduce the heat and simmer for 40 minutes or until the meat is tender, adding more water as necessary.

3 Make the sauce. Blend the cornflour with the remaining ingredients in a bowl. Stir into the lamb and mix well without breaking up the meat.

4 Add the noodles with the beans. Simmer gently until both the noodles and the beans are cooked. Add salt and pepper to taste. Divide the noodles among four large bowls, garnish each portion with half a hard-boiled egg, sprinkle with spring onions and serve.

Chicken and Prawn Hot Pot

Using a portable hot pot, this dish, known as *Yosenabe*, combines meat, fish, vegetables and noodles to create a really warming meal that is cooked at the table.

Serves 4

INGREDIENTS

400 g/14 oz chicken thighs or
    breasts on the bone
8 uncooked tiger prawns
200 g/7 oz dried udon noodles
4 shiitake mushrooms, stems
    removed
½ bunch Chinese leaves, cut into
    3-cm/1¼-in slices
3 leeks, sliced diagonally into pieces
    1 cm/½ in-thick
15 x 10-cm/6 x 4-in piece beancurd
    (about 150 g/5 oz), cut into
    3-cm/1¼-in cubes
300 g/11 oz shirataki noodles,
    boiled for 2 minutes, drained and
    halved

FOR THE YOSENABE STOCK

1 litre/1¾ pints/4 cups kombu and
    bonito stock
90 ml/6 tbsp sake or dry white wine
30 ml/2 tbsp dark soy sauce
20 ml/4 tsp mirin
10 ml/2 tsp salt

udon noodles
shiitake mushrooms
Chinese leaves
tiger prawns
chicken thighs
leeks
sake
mirin
kombu and bonito stock
beancurd
dark soy sauce

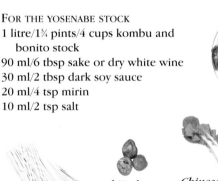 **1** Cut the chicken into 1-cm/½-in chunks. Remove the black intestinal vein from the prawns if necessary.

2 Cook the udon noodles for 2 minutes less than the packet instructions, drain and rinse thoroughly, then drain again and set aside. Arrange all the remaining ingredients on large plates.

3 Bring all the ingredients for the yosenabe stock to the boil in the hot pot. Add the chicken and simmer for 3 minutes, skimming the broth throughout cooking.

4 Add the remaining ingredients, except the udon noodles and simmer for 5 minutes or until cooked. Diners serve themselves from the simmering hot pot. Finally, when all the ingredients have been eaten, add the udon noodles to the rest of the soup, heat through and serve in bowls to round off the meal.

INDEX